Interviewing to Gather Relevant Content for Training

Interviewing to Gather Relevant Content for Training

"Good instructional designers have always been good listeners and good communicators, but it is often difficult to tell people precisely how to do this. In *Interviewing to Gather Relevant Content for Training* the interview process is carefully analyzed and systematically explained, reflecting a wealth of practical experience. While a content identification interview is complicated, detailed, and time-consuming, Gordon Shand (in the best instructional design tradition) has made it seem simple and entirely within reach."

—**Rita C. Richey, Ph.D.**, coauthor of *The Instructional Design, Knowledge Base: Theory, Research, and Practice;* Professor Emeritus, Instructional Technology, Wayne State University

"*Interviewing to Gather Relevant Content for Training* is a must have reference book for any learning and development professional tasked with identifying content for training. Gordon Shand's book dives deep into the concepts of relevant content and interviewing to give a robust and complete picture of this required skill. This book is filled with practical advice and models that are immediately applicable. The most important aspect of the book is that Shand keeps you focused on the business – something that sets this book apart from the rest!"

—**Jenn Labin**, author of *Real World Training Design* and Managing Principal of T.E.R.P. Associates

"Clearly Gordon Shand has a large amount of experience creating training. The book, *Interviewing to Gather Relevant Content for Training,* which is relevant for both technical and non-technical training, includes examples that relate to a wide range of industries and organizations. The specific questions he offers for performing a needs analysis and gathering content are a valuable addition to any training practitioner's toolkit."

—**Sarah Wakefield**, author of *Technical Training Basics*

Improving Corporate, Job, and Employee Performance

Interviewing to Gather Relevant Content for Training

... asking the right questions

Gordon D. Shand

HDC Human Development Consultants Ltd.
PO Box 4710, Edmonton, AB, Canada T6E 5G5
www.hdc.ca
www.safethink.ca

© **2015 by HDC Human Development Consultants Ltd.**

All rights reserved. No part of this publication may be reproduced, stored in a retrieval system, or transmitted in any form or by any means, electronic, mechanical, photocopying, recording, or otherwise, without the prior written permission of HDC Human Development Consultants Ltd. (HDC).

This publication is designed to provide general information regarding the subject matter covered. Care has been taken to ensure the accuracy of the information and that the instructions contained in this publication are clear and reflect sound practice. The user understands that HDC is not providing engineering services. The user understands that any procedures (task steps) that are published or referenced may have to be modified to comply with specific equipment, work conditions, company standards, company policies and practices, legislation, and user qualifications. HDC does not make any representations, guarantees, or warranties of any kind whatsoever with respect to the content hereof and the results to be achieved by implementing the procedures (task steps) herein. To the maximum extent permitted by applicable law, in no event shall HDC be liable for any damages whatsoever (including without limitation, direct or indirect damages for personal injury, damages to the environment, damages to business property, loss of business profit, or any other pecuniary loss). The use of the information and procedures (task steps) herein is undertaken at the sole risk of the user.

Library and Archives Canada Cataloguing in Publication
Shand, Gordon D.
Interviewing to gather relevant content for training: asking the right questions / Gordon D. Shand.
ISBN 978-1-55338-060-3
1. Employees—Training of. 2. Interviewing—Technique.
3. Critical thinking. I. HDC Human Development Consultants
II. Title.
HF5549.5.T7S52 2015   658.3'1243   C2015-902760-X

Published by HDC Human Development Consultants Ltd.

Published in Canada

Website: www.hdc.ca
E-mail: hdc@hdc.ca
Phone: (780) 463-3909

Acknowledgements

HDC Human Development Consultants Ltd.'s business philosophy is to cost-effectively produce quality training resources that get results for its customers. In keeping with this philosophy, HDC has developed a comprehensive training program for its consultants so that they can maintain satisfied customers. One of the training competencies is for consultants to interview subject matter experts to gather relevant content. Throughout the interviewing process, consultants are expected to provide leadership to identify and document relevant content that contributes to improved corporate, job, and employee performance. Well planned and documented content also contributes to the efficient development of training and assessment resources.

Many HDC staff have contributed to the development of the interviewing process and this book. Thanks to the consultants who worked so diligently with me to produce this book. They were adamant in adhering to our standards for quality, even when I was burned out and wanted to put closure to a topic. Thanks to Janelle Beblow, Art Deane, Alice Graham, Jean MacGregor, and Bruno Schoenfelder for the wonderful edits and feedback. Thanks to Phil Jenkins, Kris Vasey, and Denise Hodgins for developing the illustrations, formatting the documents, and creating the book covers. Thanks to Maria Peck for coordinating the work and proofing text. Their personal support, commitment to quality, and attention to detail are greatly appreciated.

 Interviewing to Gather Relevant Content for Training

Table of Contents

Foreword	ix
Training Objectives	xii
Section 1: Introduction	1

PART A Identify Relevant Content — 7

Section 2 Using Critical Thinking Strategies to Identify Relevant Content — 9

- 2.1 The Exemplary Worker Model — 10
- 2.2 Preventing Illness and Injury (Safety) — 12
- 2.3 Protect the Environment — 16
- 2.4 Use Equipment and Materials Effectively — 18
- 2.5 Use a Business Model to Understand the Organization — 24
- 2.6 Work Effectively — 34
- 2.7 Reasons, Causes, Effects, and Consequences — 48
- 2.8 *What if...?* Questions — 60
- 2.9 View Issues from Other People's Perspectives — 67

Section 3 Relevant Content Principles — 73

Section 4 Relevant Content and Instructional Design — 81

- 4.1 Structure of Training and Reference Resources — 82
- 4.2 Pitfalls in Designing and Developing Training Programs — 83

Table of Contents

PART B	**Interviewing to Gather Relevant Content**	**105**
	Benefits of Interviewing	106
	Drawbacks of Interviewing	107
	Importance of Effective Interviewing	108
Section 5	Planning Interviewing Sessions	111
5.1	Selecting the SME	112
5.2	Preparing the SME for the Interview	113
5.3	Preparing for the Interview	113
Section 6	Conducting the Interview	119
Major Step 1—Set up the Work Area		120
Major Step 2—Explain the Training Program		122
Major Step 3—Describe the Interviewing Process		125
Major Step 4—Gather the Content		133
Major Step 5—Refine the Content		166
Section 7	Using SMEs Who are not Part of the Group Receiving Training	169
Section 8	The Consultant's Role	171
Section 9	Summary	175
Section 10	Suggested Exercises	181

Interviewing to Gather Relevant Content for Training

Table of Contents (continued)

Attachments

Attachment 1—	Purpose and Benefits of Interviewing the Customer's Experienced Staff	A1-1
Attachment 2—	Project and Interview Preparation Checklists	A2-1
Attachment 3—	Interviewing Checklist	A3-1
Attachment 4—	Examples of Module Outlines for Content Gathering (sometimes called Expanded Scope)	A4-1
Attachment 5—	Shot Sheet	A5-1
Attachment 6—	Relevant Content Questions	A6-1

Foreword

Designing training materials (like old age) is not for sissies. It is a complicated, very detailed, and time consuming endeavor. Moreover, if it's done right, the products should look simple. Gordon Shand has tackled one of the critical phases of instructional design – content identification – and produced a clear, step-by-step procedure for one approach to this task. This book teaches designers how to lead interviews with subject matter experts, guiding them through the process of specifying training content that is relevant and comprehensive.

There are ways, other than expert interviewing, to identify the content of a training program; job analysis and task analysis are two other approaches that readily lead to training-relevant job tasks and their component parts. However, designers of all theoretical bents have also long relied upon content which has been explained by those currently on the job. One of the most important reasons for using the interview approach is that the content becomes infused with context, often revealing details that were previously unknown. For example, the content can be described in light of the target organization's culture. While learning about the content, designers at the same time can learn things such as the typical practice in a given company, the lingo used, the equipment involved. Content defined through the interview process also can be described in conjunction with descriptions of the people who will be employing the new knowledge and skills. The designer can learn of attitudes, concerns, and backgrounds of both those who will be participating in the forthcoming training and their supervisors. Thus, a good interview (unlike other content identification approaches) yields not only precise content, but also critical elements of the contextual and learner analyses.

A concomitant outcome of content-identification interviews is the personal involvement of clients in the instructional design process. User-centered design techniques facilitate organizations taking ownership of the resulting training programs, no small matter when external consultants are hired to produce the instruction.

Good instructional designers have always been good listeners and good communicators, but it is often difficult to tell people precisely how to do this. Interviewing to Gather Relevant Content for Training accomplishes the task. The interview process is carefully analyzed and systematically explained. In addition, it is apparent that the content of this book reflects a wealth of practical experience. Common pitfalls are noted, and very useful cautions are interjected throughout. Often these are basic, common sense warnings that we all need to keep in mind, such as "don't forget to back-up and save your files".

Finally, this book has a general "performance improvement" orientation; it is directed towards not only improvement of the employee's on-the-job performance, but that of the organization as a whole. As such, this book is geared to understanding the nature of a given organization and responding to its needs. The superior interview is seen as a product of critical thinking strategies that, in effect, lead one through a complete analysis of the organization as a system. Thus, the effective interview is contextualized and the effective interviewer completes the task with a high level of site-specific knowledge.

The content identification interview indeed is complicated, detailed, and time-consuming, but Gordon Shand (in the best instructional design tradition) has made it seem simple and entirely within reach.

Rita C. Richey
Professor Emeritus
Instructional Technology
Wayne State University

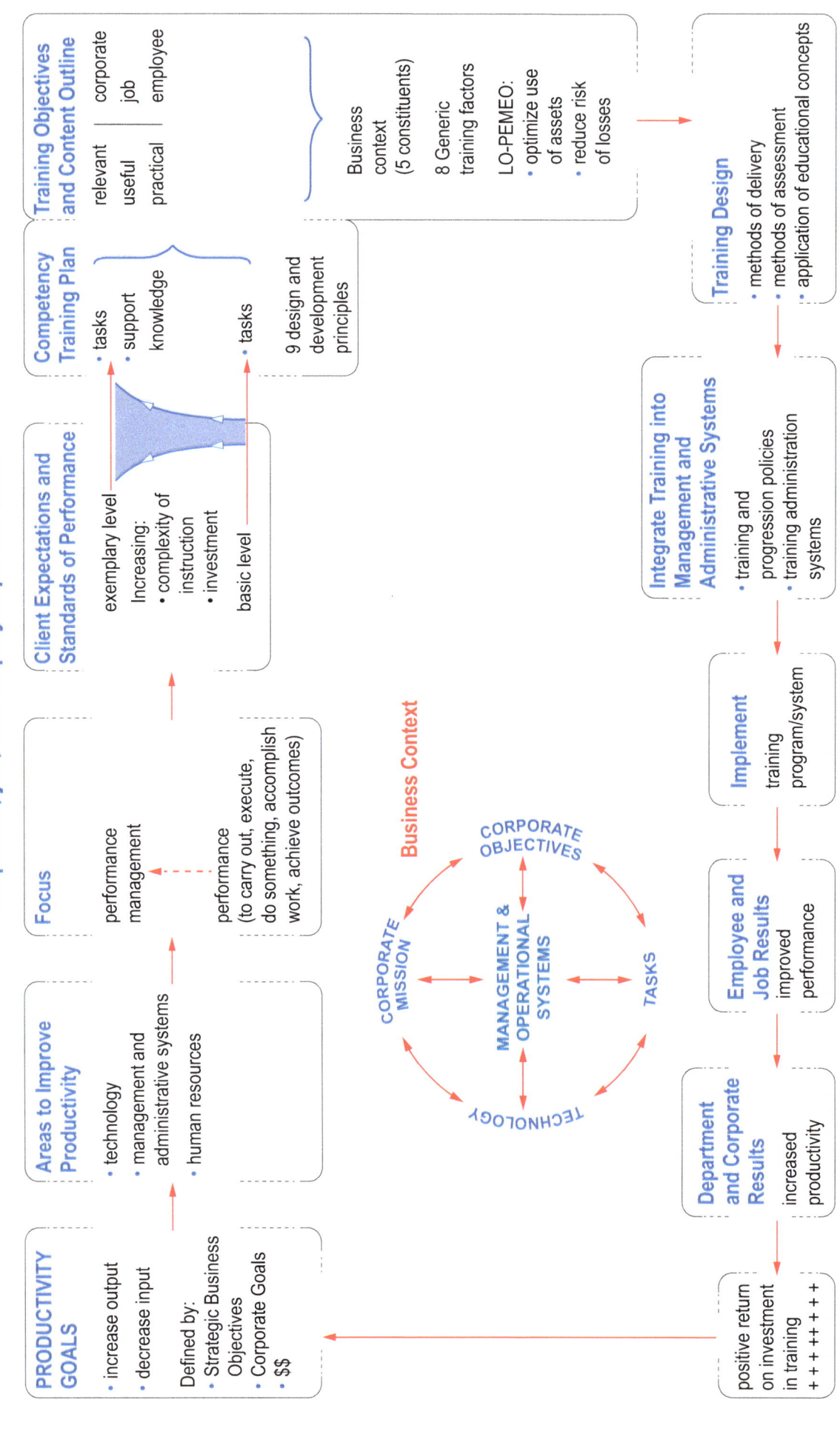

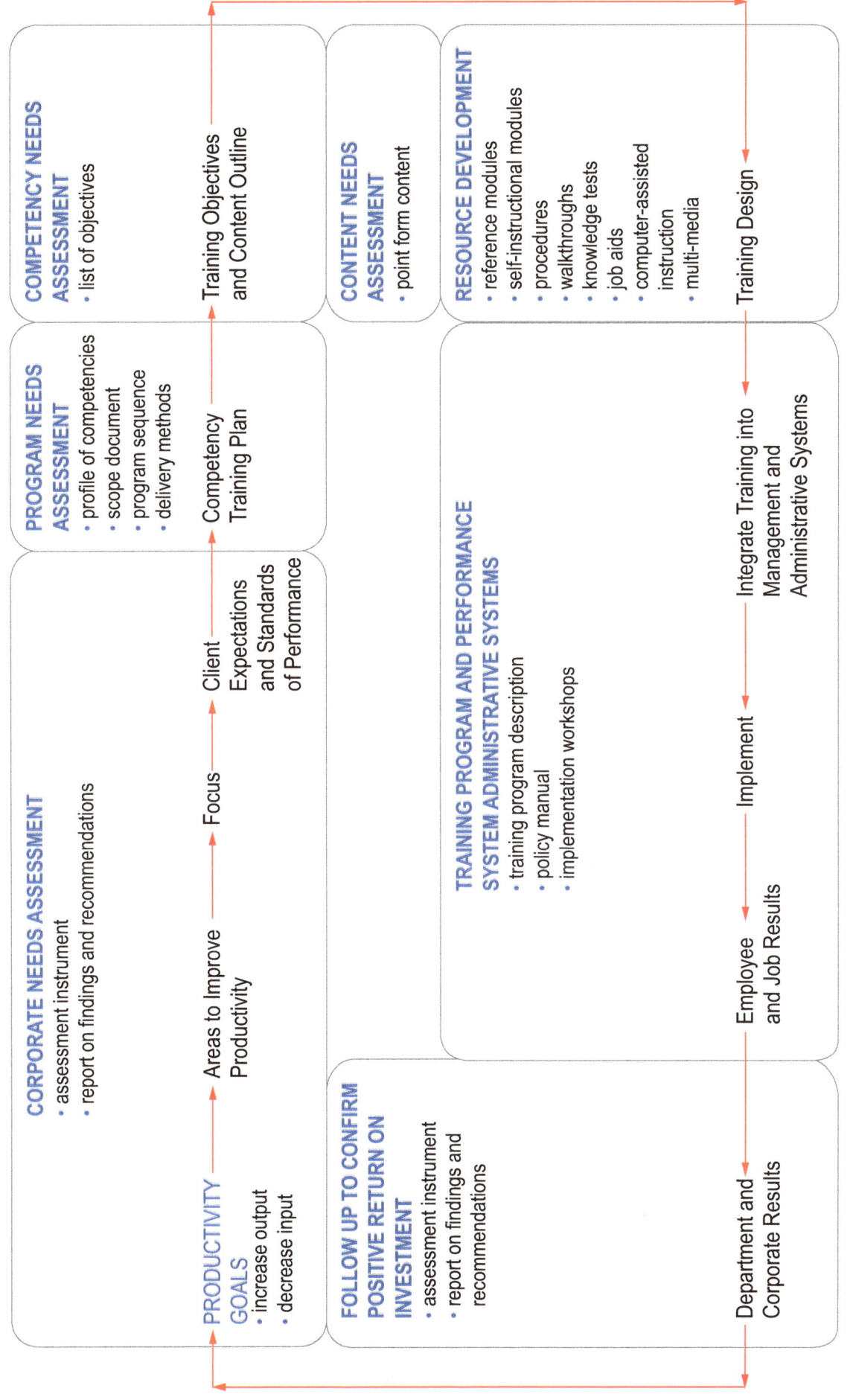

Training Objectives

Upon completion of this book, you will be able to:

Part A: Identify Relevant Content
- Describe criteria and critical thinking strategies to identify relevant content
- Describe relevant content principles
- Describe the relationship between relevant content and instructional design

Part B: Interview to Gather Relevant Content
- Describe the importance, benefits, and drawbacks of the interview process
- Plan interview sessions
- Conduct interviews
  - Set up the work area
  - Explain the training program
  - Describe the interview process
  - Gather the content
  - Refine the content
- Describe the consultant's role when interviewing customer staff

Section 1

Introduction

This book is for training development consultants and technical writers who may have different roles:
- work for a consulting firm that provides training development services for other organizations and is independent of its customers
- provide internal support for an organization
- are self-employed (freelance consultants or writers)

As a training development consultant or technical writer, your single most important task is to identify relevant content for resources you are developing.

Relevant content contributes to business success by improving your customer's employee, job, and corporate performance. Training and reference resources that contain content that is relevant, useful, and practical help employees work safely, effectively, and efficiently.

With effective consulting and instructional design and development processes, you can develop quality training for a variety of disciplines and technologies. To do so, you must provide **leadership** when working with Subject Matter Experts (SMEs) to identify content important for training.

Part A of this book focuses on how to use generic thinking strategies and ask critical questions to identify content that is relevant, useful, and practical. Thinking strategies are included because they provide the foundation for effective interviewing. Part A also describes the relationship between relevant content and instructional design.

Part B focuses on how to plan and conduct interviews to gather and structure relevant content so that:
- you can write effective training and reference resources (such as self-instructional modules), knowledge test items, and procedures
- your training and reference resources will help to improve people's performance

Because this book includes descriptions of critical thinking strategies (Part A) that can be used to gather relevant content, it is quite long and may make you think that the interviewing process is more complex than it actually is. However, when the interviewing steps are listed and grouped into sections, the interviewing process (Part B) is quite linear.

HDC Human Development Consultants Ltd. (HDC) has been developing customized training programs for more than twenty-six years. Most of the suggestions in this book are based on our consultants' collective experiences interviewing to gather relevant training content.

For ease of writing, this book focuses on training consultants and technical writers working for a consulting firm that provides training design and development services to other organizations. The concepts, however, apply equally well to those who provide internal services or are self-employed.

The primary focus of this book is on interviewing SMEs to identify and document relevant, useful, and practical content that will contribute to improved corporate, job, and employee performance.

Introduction

The interviewing processes described in this book can be adapted to many instructional program development models. In the front of this book, HDC's *Training and Performance Model* has been included for those who design and develop training programs to provide a training program development context for gathering content.

Some of the **preconditions** for gathering content are:
- a general training management plan has been developed
- the plan may include incentives such as a pay-and-progression scheme and/or career development paths
- training resource ownership and confidentiality agreements may be in place
- the customer's business context is known
- whether or not trainees have access to high speed internet
- the audience(s) and their roles and responsibilities have been defined
- the audience and their characteristics/qualifications have been identified
- it has been determined if language and literacy is a barrier
- it has been determined whether the training will be delivered at a single site or at multiple sites
- whether the audience works with others or alone
- the competencies (or general training objectives) have been identified
- the competencies have been specified as being generic for one or more disciplines, discipline specific, or site-specific for a discipline
- the competencies have been grouped and the groups sequenced for training progression
- within each competency group, the competencies may or may not be sequenced
- the critical content (e.g., safety, equipment reliability, public image) for each competency may or may not be documented
- there is most likely an understanding of the methods of delivery (e.g., self-instruction, computer-assisted instruction, video, leader-lead workshops, one-on-one mentoring)
- whether the training will be delivered during the work day or after work

- the training for a task and the required support knowledge will be delivered at about the same time
- for each competency, methods of assessment (e.g., knowledge, job performance) may or may not be documented)

Outcomes of the interviewing process include:
- the content is documented in point form
- the content may or may not be categorized in objective terms (e.g., conditions, resources, performance, standards)

> **NOTE** The interviewing process description that follows is for self-instruction (paper-based or electronic notebook). Self-instruction is chosen because of the various delivery media/methods; self-instruction usually requires the most detailed content to be gathered. The gathered content can be adapted for other delivery methods.

- the content can be prescriptive or descriptive, depending on the desired outcomes
- limited educational principles are documented:
  - the content is grouped and sequenced in a way that will most likely be suitable for structuring the content of the delivery medium
  - content for the introduction is documented (advanced organizer)
  - other educational principles will be incorporated when developing the delivery medium. For example:
    - transitions
    - flow drawings
    - illustrations
    - icons
    - analogies

Terms

This book uses the following terms:

boilerplate	standard text template that can be used as is or changed slightly for different applications
competency	the skill and knowledge required to effectively perform a specific task
curriculum	a set of courses or program of study
employee	generic term for someone working for an organization. This book uses the term employee to refer to those who are workers, foremen, and supervisors.
instructional design	the process used to design instruction and learning activities. The fundamental steps in the instructional design process are: • analyze the learner • identify the competencies/general training objectives • develop the evaluation instruments • develop the instructional materials (training manuals, self-instructional modules, videos, slide shows, etc.) • develop the instructional process.
job *(broad definition)*	a job is what one does for a living. The term reflects the type of work one does and may be equivalent to one's occupation (e.g., electrician).
job *(narrow definition)*	the term job is often used to mean a specific work assignment or unit of work. The job has a beginning and an end, as in, *When you have completed that job, come and see me.* This book uses the narrow definition of the term job.

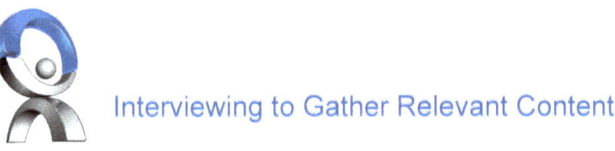

performance	doing something, carrying out an activity or action, executing, accomplishing work, achieving objectives, achieving outcomes, achieving results. The term can have different meanings, depending on the level within the organization to which the term applies: corporate, job, or line worker.
profile	a diagram or spreadsheet showing all the competencies of a training program and their relationship to one another
scope	a detailed outline of the content required for each competency in the profile
Subject Matter Expert (SME)	the person you will be interviewing to gather relevant content
task	a unit of work that has a beginning and an end. A skill is the ability to do the unit of work. Support knowledge is the knowledge required to do the task safely, effectively, and efficiently. Support knowledge is required to be able to perform at an exemplary level, solve problems, and make effective decisions in the best interest of the organization.
worker	line worker. Someone who performs tasks (e.g., constructing, operating, diagnosing, or maintaining tasks).

PART A

Identify Relevant Content

Your customers expect that the training you develop will be relevant, useful, and practical and contribute to effective employee, job, and corporate performance. They expect training to address issues important to their business success; for example, the expectation is that employees are able to do their jobs safely, effectively, and efficiently.

One of the most critical issues affecting the training is the *level of performance* the customer wants their employees to achieve. For example:

- Entry level training focuses on performing tasks: *Do as I tell you and show you, and don't ask why.*
- Exemplary level training focuses on performing tasks *exceptionally well* and making *effective decisions* in the best interest of the organization. Exemplary employees have support knowledge about equipment operation, materials, safety, and the environment. They also have knowledge about the reasons, causes, effects, consequences, indicators, and desired responses to abnormal situations.

Different customers can have different levels of expectations for employee performance, ranging from entry level to

exemplary level. Developing training that is not at the level expected by the customer causes customer dissatisfaction:

- Training targeted at too high a level increases development costs dramatically.
- Training targeted at a level below the customer's expectations results in employees who are not able to perform to the customer's satisfaction.

Section 2

Using Critical Thinking Strategies to Identify Relevant Content

The most important concern for customers is that training content helps employees do their jobs well (i.e., the training is relevant and contributes to improving employee, job, and corporate performance). Often, you will identify the training content by interviewing Subject Matter Experts (SMEs). During the interview, you need to provide leadership to identify the *relevant* content because SMEs often struggle to determine what content to include or not include in the training. You can effectively provide this leadership to identify relevant content by using critical thinking strategies and asking specific types of question.

This section provides a brief description of key critical thinking strategies you can use to identify relevant training content. These critical thinking strategies are based upon *The Exemplary Worker* series of books. These books focus on critical thinking strategies that exemplary workers use to perform their jobs effectively. The critical thinking strategies are generic and apply to most disciplines and workplaces.

NOTE *The Exemplary Worker* series of books was developed from HDC's internal training program. The goal of the internal training program is for consultants to be able to identify and develop training that adds value for customers and contributes to the customer's business success. Most of the critical thinking strategies in the internal training program were identified by working with exemplary workers to gather training content.

The Exemplary Worker series is for anyone who wants to be an exemplary performer or who wants to refine his or her skills. Section 2 of this book provides an overview of the critical thinking strategies addressed more thoroughly in *The Exemplary Worker* series and identifies how to apply these strategies when you are gathering content and designing and developing training. The books are referenced because you may feel that you need descriptions of the strategies that are more comprehensive than those provided in this book.

2.1 The Exemplary Worker Model

The *exemplary worker model* is a framework for the critical thinking strategies that follow.

LO-PEMEO™
Loss and **O**ptimization of
People
Equipment
Materials
Environment
Organization

Organizations want to optimize production and minimize losses. At the job level, the primary optimization and loss concerns are for five domains: **P**eople, **E**quipment, **M**aterials, the **E**nvironment, and the **O**rganization (PEMEO). There is a potential for optimization and loss to each domain. Combining optimization and loss control with PEMEO creates a model and strategy for identifying relevant content (LO-PEMEO). For example:
- LP (Loss to People) is illness and injury
- OP (Optimizing People's performance) is working effectively and efficiently.
- LE (Loss to Equipment) is damage to equipment and shortening of equipment life

Furthermore, the work environment is defined by the *conditions, actions*, and *events* within the workplace that affect PEMEO.

PART A Section 2
Using Critical Thinking Strategies to Identify Relevant Content

The following table summarizes the themes of the *exemplary worker model* and identifies the related titles in *The Exemplary Worker* series.

Themes	Exemplary Worker Book Titles
L-P Loss to People (Safety)	*SafeThink* Identify, predict, and control hazardous situations.
O-P Optimize People's Performance	*WorkThink* Work effectively and efficiently.
LO-E Loss and Optimization of Equipment	*EquipThink* Use tools and equipment effectively and efficiently.
LO-M Loss and Optimization of Materials	*MatThink* Use materials effectively and efficiently.
LO-E Loss and Optimization of the Environment	*EnviroThink* Protect the environment.
LO-O Loss and Optimization of the Organization	*JobThink* Contribute to job and corporate performance.
LO-PEMEO Use thinking strategies for the workplace	*MetaThink* Integrate thinking strategies for exemplary performance.

LO-PEMEO provides a framework for asking quality questions. By asking questions and seeking answers from the SME for some of the questions, you identify relevant content for training. The big question is: What questions should I ask?

When starting to interview an SME, you can ask general questions that relate to the *exemplary worker model*. For example:
- *Are there any safety issues before, during, or after performing the task?*
- *What is most important to doing this task effectively?*
- *How can the worker harm the equipment?*
- *How can the worker optimize the performance of the equipment?*

- *How can the worker make the most use of the materials?*
- *How can the materials be damaged?*
- *How can the environment be threatened?*
- *How can the worker best do the task to contribute to the overall job and business success?*
- *What are the reasons for...?*
- *What causes...?*
- *What are the consequences?*
- *What are the indicators for...?*
- *What is the worker's response if...?*

The questions relating to LO-PEMEO help you to ask many of the right questions to identify relevant content for training.

You can provide further leadership by asking more specific questions. First ask yourself the question to determine if it may be relevant and, if so, ask the SME.

The following subsections describe some critical thinking strategies that help you identify relevant content and determine what content is **not** relevant. The critical thinking strategies help you to think through the work that must be captured in the training program. The thinking strategies are generic so that they apply to all types of industry, jobs, and work environments. Specific questions you can ask that relate to each strategy are also identified.

2.2 Preventing Illness and Injury (Safety)

Safety is always a concern for your customers. No organization wants workers to be injured. Workplace regulations hold all levels of the organization responsible for implementing effective safety programs.

To perform a task safely, workers must identify all potential hazards (agents of cause) that exist before work starts, could arise during the work, or remain after the work is completed.

When potential hazards are identified, workers must take steps to effectively control the hazards to prevent illness or injury.

PART A Section 2
Using Critical Thinking Strategies to Identify Relevant Content

Ambient

For this strategy, ambient conditions are those conditions that are ideal for human existence such as room temperature, adequate light, and minimum noise.

Non-ambient

Non-ambient conditions are those conditions that cause discomfort.

Conditions:

the nature of the workplace, includes physical surroundings, quality of atmosphere, status of equipment operation, and nature of the work being performed

Actions:

worker's activities required to perform a task

Events:

planned and unplanned happenings such as a temporary shutdown of a mill for repair or a pressurized vessel rupture

There are six categories of hazard. When identifying relevant content, you can ask the SME these general questions to identify the categories involved in the task:
- *Does the work involve hazardous materials?*
- *Does the work involve objects, motion, or force that could cause harm?*
- *Does the work involve non-ambient conditions that could cause harm?*
- *Is current or static electricity a factor in doing the work?*
- *Is radiation present when doing the work?*
- *Could changes lead to or create a hazardous situation?*

A very important feature of *SafeThink* that makes identifying hazards effective and efficient is the use of generalities. For example, all rotating objects (e.g., shaft, fan, egg beater) can be hazardous.

Just because a hazard is present, or will be created while carrying out a task, does not mean that workers are at risk of illness or injury. For example, a chemical that is flammable and toxic stored in the original container in a fire cabinet does not pose a threat to workers in the area. However, if a worker removes the chemical container from the cabinet and carries it to the work area, a potentially hazardous situation can be created. The interaction of a hazard and the workplace ***conditions, actions***, and ***events*** creates the hazardous situation.

If the SME answers *yes* to any of the six general hazard questions, your next question will be: Are there any ***conditions, actions***, or ***events*** that can lead to or create a hazardous situation?

Interviewing to Gather Relevant Content for Training

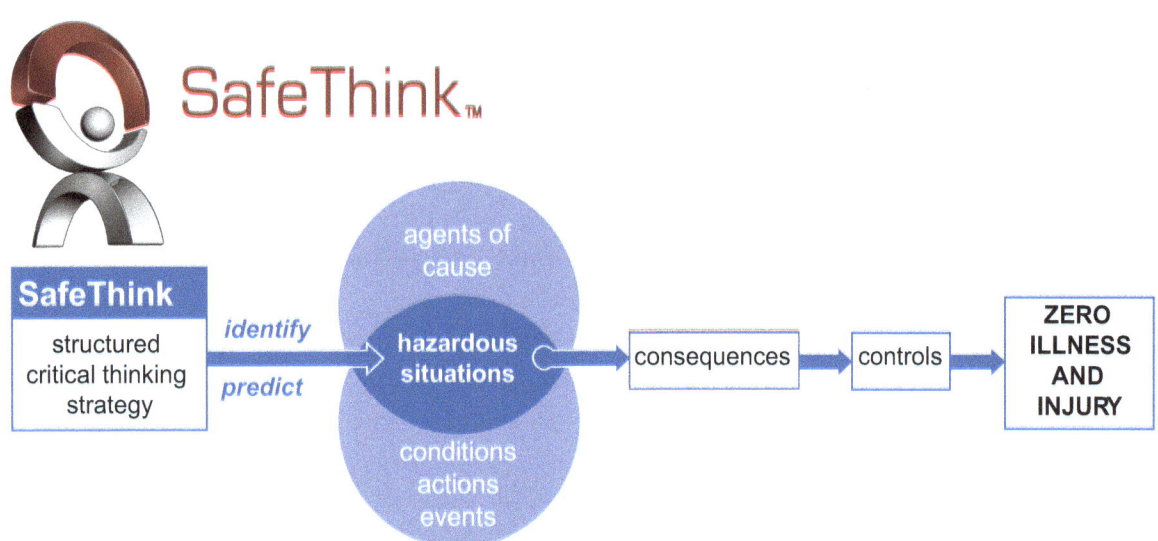

A hazardous situation is created as a result of the interaction of a hazard (agent of cause) and a condition, action, or event.

If the SME says *yes* to your question about conditions, actions or events, ask the following questions:
- *What are the potential consequences of the hazardous situation?*
- *What controls can be used to reduce the probability of an incident occurring and/or the severity of consequences?*

The Exemplary Worker book *SafeThink* provides an in-depth explanation about using the critical thinking strategy to identify, predict, and control hazardous situations.

Identify hazardous situations

This learning activity helps you refine the questions you ask the SME to identify and predict hazardous situations.

Before, during, and after performing a task, conditions, actions, and events can lead to or create a hazardous situation. To complete this exercise:
- identify a task that you could perform at work or at home
- list the conditions, actions, and events associated with each category of hazard that makes the work potentially hazardous.

PART A Section 2
Using Critical Thinking Strategies to Identify Relevant Content

Not all categories may apply to a specific task and, in the workplace environment, there may be only one condition, or action, or event that creates a hazardous situation.

Here is an example: the task of re-painting a room in your house. Before painting, you need to move some of the furniture out of the room and move other furniture to the middle of the room and cover them up. After the painting is complete, you must clean up the tools and put the furniture in place.

The task is: <u>*Re-paint a room in your house.*</u>

Category of Hazard	Conditions, actions, events *before* the task	Conditions, actions, events *while* doing the task	Conditions, actions, events *after* doing the task
Hazardous Material	None	Fumes from paint could be toxic. Paint can splash into eyes.	Fumes from paint and solvent could be toxic.
Objects, Motion, Force	Furniture and corners of door openings can create points of contact. Moving furniture can cause strains.	Furniture in room can be source of impact or tripping. Standing on stool is potential for falling.	Furniture and corners of door openings can create points of contact. Moving furniture can cause strains.
Non-Ambient Conditions	None	Paint aerosols	None
Current and/or Static Electricity	Electrical switches and receptacle plates removed and electrical components taped. Possible contact with electrical connections if electricity not turned off.	Possible contact with electrical connections if electricity not shut off.	When removing tape, possible contact with electrical connections if electricity not turned off.
Radiation	None	If spotlights used for extra lighting, lights can temporarily blind.	None
Changes	Furniture in different location can be source of impact.	Furniture in different location can be source of impact.	None

Interviewing to Gather Relevant Content for Training

Now try a different task.

The task is: _____

Category of Hazard	Conditions, actions, events *before* the task	Conditions, actions, events *while* doing the task	Conditions, actions, events *after* doing the task
Hazardous Material			
Objects, Motion, Force			
Non-Ambient Conditions			
Current and/or Static Electricity			
Radiation			
Changes			

2.3 Protect the Environment

The public and organizations have a heightened concern for protecting the natural environment. Regulators hold all levels of the organization responsible for implementing effective environmental protection programs. Environmental and safety issues are often related; if a material (gas, liquid, or solid) can harm the environment, it might also harm people.

Exemplary workers ask eleven general questions relating to the environment. The specific wording of the questions depends on the type of work being performed or on the technical process.

For most tasks, ask the SME the following nine questions:
- *Can this material cause harm to the environment?*
- *How do I store this material safely?*

PART A Section 2
Using Critical Thinking Strategies to Identify Relevant Content

- *How do I dispose of this material safely?*
- *How much material can be released, disposed of, or harvested without harming the environment?*
- *How are pollutant releases measured or monitored?*
- *What technical controls are being used to limit environmental impact?*
- *How do I know release rates are being exceeded?*
- *What do I do if release rates are exceeded?*
- *What do I do if there is a spill of material that has the potential to harm the environment?*

The Exemplary Worker book *EnviroThink* provides an in-depth explanation of the key environmental issues.

Protect the environment

This learning activity helps you refine the questions you ask the SME to identify environmental issues.

Many actions have the potential of impacting the environment. For example, when washing dishes, the drained soap and grease are disposed of in the water in lakes and rivers. A city can discharge large amounts of treated waste water which can still affect aquatic life. In a home, waste water is discharged sporadically but the city discharges waste water continuously.

In the following table, state a task or job that you do at work or at home which could impact the environment. Complete the table to determine how the task affects the environment.

Your task or job	Action on the environment	Which environmental component is affected	Is the impact continuous or sporadic?	Specific effect on environment
	☐ remove ☐ add ☐ modify	☐ air ☐ water ☐ land	☐ continous ☐ sporadic	

2.4 Use Equipment and Materials Effectively

Two other domains of LO-PEMEO are equipment and materials. Note that, in the model, equipment is stated with the understanding that tools are also included. Materials also include components used to make things or repair equipment.

There is a set of related issues affecting the effective use of equipment and materials. When working with equipment, the main concern is to control *changes* through work and technical processes to achieve the desired results (quality). The following diagram shows the three stages of the *change* process:

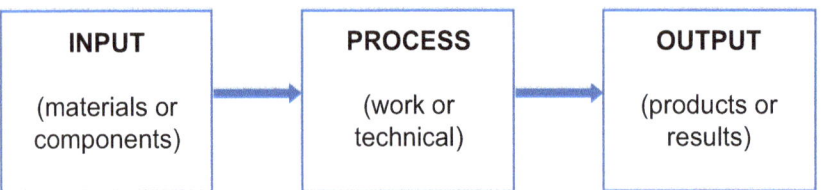

As a generality, work and technical processes are used to change materials to produce a desired result (e.g., reshape metal, cut glass to size, assemble an appliance, separate hydrocarbons into various components, create a chemical change). Generally, it is desirable that the quality of the output product remain constant. Sometimes a change in the quality of the input materials creates the need to adjust the work or technical process to achieve the desired results.

You can use the *input, process*, and *output* thinking strategy in three different sequences:
- input–process–output
- output–process–input
- output–input–process

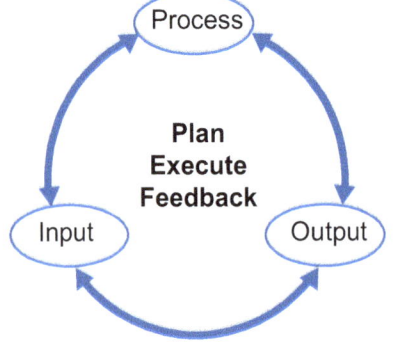

Think of *input, process*, and *output* as a continuous loop.

PART A Section 2
Using Critical Thinking Strategies to Identify Relevant Content

Start at any point in the loop and go in either direction to gain an understanding of the technology and process used to achieve the desired results. After you have used the strategy to initially think through the work, you may find yourself using a different starting point and sequence to get a better understanding of a specific concern.

Each stage of the change process has variables:
- **input variables** define the quality of the materials used
- **process variables** define the tools and equipment that create the change
- **output variables** define the quality of the product or results

Measuring Variables

Variables relate to properties, characteristics, or settings. Units of measure are used to define the quality of the input, process, and output variables (e.g., temperature, pressure, volume, mass).

Material properties: scientifically defined qualities such as composition, density, and melting point

Variables can be measured numerically or non-numerically:
- **numerical measurements** may be expressed as a unit value or ratio:
  - units of measurement (e.g., pressure of 100 kPa or 7 psi, power of 1865 watts or 2.5 horse power, 800 revolutions per minute)
  - ratio or percentage (e.g., 1:15 ratio of fuel to air, 12% bleach by weight)
- **non-numerical measurements** are expressed in terms of our senses. For example:
  - a liquid looks cloudy instead of clear
  - the surface of a board appears rough instead of smooth
  - apply enough force to obtain a clean cut but not enough to overload the motor

Material characteristics: size, shape, surface finish, type of break such as splintering that can often be controlled by the manufacturer

Input, process, and output variables have target values or optimal ranges. For example:
- the lumber must be less than 50 mm thick
- use a #2 Robertson screwdriver
- set the rpm to 1200
- torque the bolts to 30 foot pounds

Interviewing to Gather Relevant Content for Training

- the temperature of the adhesive must be above 15°C
- control the pressure of the gas entering the vessel between 500 kPa and 575 kPa
- the width of the material must be 20 mm, ± 1 mm
- the optimal composition of the product is 40% A, 60% B

Classification of Variables

A variable can be classified according to its state and controllability:

- either static or dynamic (state)
- either controllable or non-controllable (controllability)

static variable a variable that cannot be easily changed (e.g., the hardness of oak lumber).

dynamic variable a variable that can easily change (e.g., wind velocity, the number of orders).

controllable variable a variable that you or technology can change (e.g., the rpm of an engine, the depth of cut of a milling machine, the dimensions of plywood parts).

non-controllable variable a variable that cannot be easily regulated (e.g., the frequency of customer orders).

The two categories (state and controllability) of a variable combine to produce four possible types of variable as shown in the following illustration:

Variable	Static	Dynamic
Controllable	static and controllable	dynamic and controllable
Non-Controllable	static and non-controllable	dynamic and non-controllable

Knowing whether an equipment or material variable can change and whether or not the worker can control the change is very helpful in doing the job well and responding effectively to changes. Cause or reason for changes and how changes can impact PEMEO (i.e., LO-PEMEO) must also be understood.

The *type* of variable can have a significant impact on the loss and optimization of PEMEO, and on the decisions and responses that workers make (within their limits of authority). There are many output, input, and process variables. However, the variables that are important to the work (and relative content) are the variables that the worker must deal with within his or her roles and responsibilities.

The use of variables is very useful for identifying relevant content for many different types of technology and tasks. The concept of variables can also be used for many applications other than equipment. For example, variables can be applied when using computer software. Here is an example of identifying variables for word processing software. Leaders, such as bullets, for a list of items in a document can have several variables:
- **shape** (round or square bullet, arrow, box)
- **size** (default or customized)
- **space** between the leader and first letter (default or customized)
- **indent** (no indent, default indent, or customized)

When interviewing the SME, you need to consider questions that relate to the output, input, and work or technical process. Here are some examples of questions you could first ask yourself and, if the questions seem relevant, ask the SME:

Output
- *What output variables define the quality of results?*
- *How are the output variables measured?*
- *What is the impact of the output materials on PEMEO and vice versa?*

Input
- *What are the input variables?*
- *What input variables are changed by the work or technical process?*
- *What input variables must not change?*
- *For each variable, is it static or dynamic, controllable or non-controllable?*

Work or Technical Process
- *What process variables change the materials?*
- *Are the process variables that change the materials static or dynamic, controllable or non-controllable?*
- *Which process variables can downgrade the materials?*
- *How can the materials affect equipment condition and life?*
- *How can the equipment be operated to perform effectively and efficiently?*

Change
- *How do I know an output, input, or process variable has changed?*
- *How does the change affect PEMEO?*
- *What do I do if a variable changes?*

Two *Exemplary Worker* books provide comprehensive explanations on using *output-input-process variables* thinking to contribute to employee, job, and corporate performance:
- *EquipThink* to optimize the use of equipment and extend equipment life
- *MatThink* to maximize the use of materials and minimize waste throughout a material's life cycle, from mining to refining to manufacturing, and the installation and disposal of products

Use equipment and materials effectively

This learning activity helps you refine the questions you ask of the SME to identify ways to use equipment and materials effectively.

On the following table, select a work or technical process and answer the questions.

PART A Section 2
Using Critical Thinking Strategies to Identify Relevant Content

The work or technical process is: _____

Questions	Answers
Output • What output variables define the quality of results? • How are the output variables measured? • What is the impact of the output materials on PEMEO and vice versa?	• • •
Input • What are the input variables? • What input variables are changed by the work or technical process? • What input variables must not change? • For each variable, is it static or dynamic, controllable or non-controllable?	• • • •
Work or Technical Process • What process variables change the materials? • Are the process variables that change the materials static or dynamic, controllable or non-controllable? • What process variables can downgrade the materials? • How can the materials affect equipment condition and life? • How can the equipment be operated to perform effectively and efficiently?	• • • • •
Change • How do I know an output, input, or process variable has changed? • How does the change affect PEMEO? • What do I do if a variable changes?	• • •

2.5 Use a Business Model to Understand the Organization

You need an understanding of the organization so that you can design and develop training that reflects the way the organization does business and has excellent value for your customer. One way to gain this understanding is to use thinking strategies used by exemplary workers.

Exemplary workers understand what is important to their organizations. They know the issues critical to business success and where to focus their efforts. Exemplary workers need an understanding of their organizations to perform effectively and make decisions in the best interest of their organizations. The following business model provides a practical way for you (and for exemplary workers) to understand organizations.

Business Model

The following business model is a practical approach to learn about an organization.

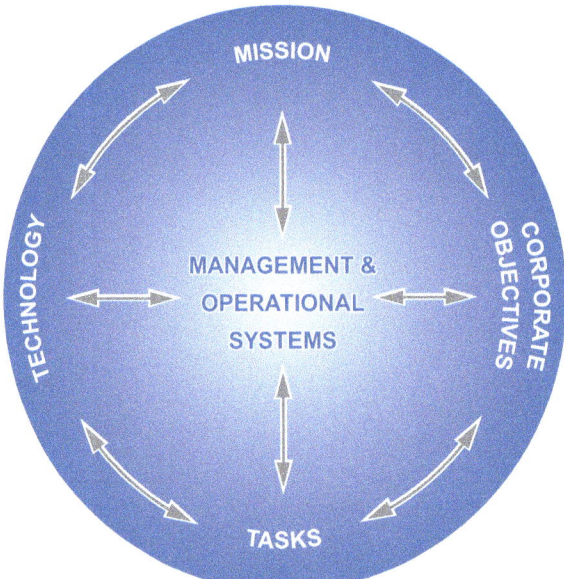

The illustration identifies some key constituents (e.g., mission, technology) of an organization. There are important relationships between constituents. The mission defines the line of business. If the line of business is a service, then performing tasks is the main way to generate revenue, and tools and equipment provide support for carrying out the work. If the line of business is to use *technology* to make products, then the technology dictates many of the tasks.

The line of business can affect the content of the resources you develop. If the line of business uses complex, automated technology (e.g., chemical manufacturing), the content you gather will most likely provide a detailed explanation on how the technology operates and how to operate the technology. If the line of business is a service, the content will most likely place a strong emphasis on how to perform tasks and less emphasis on describing tools and how the equipment operates.

Having technology and workers to perform the tasks is essential but not sufficient for business success. Workers and technology must be managed effectively by management and operational systems. The content you gather may address the importance of coordinating work and emphasize organization-specific policies and practices to follow.

Corporate Objectives

Corporate objectives are fundamental to exemplary performance because they define what is important to the organization, the job, and workers. Corporate objectives provide workers with criteria to work effectively and efficiently and make decisions in the best interest of their organizations. The corporate objectives provide direction for using technology, performing tasks, and coordinating work to effectively achieve the corporate mission. The following table lists areas commonly addressed by corporate objectives.

Areas addressed by Corporate Objectives	
• safety	• loss control
• environment	• cost control
• legislation	• customer satisfaction
• equipment reliability and life	• public image
• equipment optimization	• public disruption
• energy use	• reputation
• quality	• communication
• waste control	• teamwork

For a specific organization, a list of corporate objectives can be generated by expanding the organization's strategic business objectives or by using LO-PEMEO. Some companies issue strategic business objectives to provide direction to management and workers on where to put their energy and focus for business success. Strategic business objectives identify what the organization must do well to be successful. For example, leaders in an organization may believe it is essential for business success to provide reliable service and have satisfied customers. A department within the organization may expand this list of objectives (or goals) to address issues specific to that department's mandate.

Each of the items in the previous table relates to one or more of the LO-PEMEO domains. For example, (LP) Loss to People (safety) and (OE) Optimize Equipment. Cost control and customer satisfaction (OO) Optimize Organization.

Corporate Objectives and Instructional Design

Relevant, useful, and practical training is driven by, supports, and reinforces corporate objectives.

Corporate objectives provide a **formal link** between organizational goals and worker performance. Training must have a job application (i.e., performing *tasks*) and help workers make good *decisions* in the best interest of their organizations. But not all tasks and all decisions are of equal importance. If the tasks and decisions do not have a significant impact on the corporate objectives, then training should not be developed for those tasks and decisions. Conversely, if tasks and decisions have a significant impact on corporate objectives, then training should be developed for those tasks and decisions. The training then supports and reinforces the corporate objectives.

For designing and developing relevant, useful, and practical training, corporate objectives provide criteria for:

- selecting competencies (skills and support knowledge)
- identifying relevant content for each competency (scope document)
- establishing useful training objectives
- identifying relevant content for training (often gathered by interviewing SMEs)
- conducting a critical task analysis
- developing procedures
- selecting knowledge test items

PART A Section 2
Using Critical Thinking Strategies to Identify Relevant Content

If you are not given a list of corporate objectives before interviewing the SME, try to obtain a list of strategic business objectives. During the interview to gather content, you can use the list of strategic business objectives as a means to identify issues critical to effective performance.

Part B—*Interviewing to Gather Relevant Content* explains how to use a list of corporate objectives to identify critical issues affecting employee, job, and corporate performance. The list also helps determine the *nice to know* information that should not be gathered.

Some key questions you can ask yourself are:
- *What job performance issues are critical to the organization?*
- *What is critical to doing the work in a way that contributes to business performance?*
- *Does the worker have to know this to do the work?*
- *Does the worker need to know this to do the work to the established standards?*

Business Strategies

When identifying relevant content, it is important to keep the constituents of the business model in mind, especially business strategies and philosophy. Organizations often have business strategies to meet their missions and be competitive in the market place. For example, some organizations produce low quality, low-priced products, while others produce high quality, high-priced products. An organization may want to minimize the maintenance at a facility because it plans on mothballing the facility or may want to have a comprehensive maintenance program to keep the facility productive for many years. The business strategy also affects the amount of training, the specific content, and detail of content in the training resources you develop. The business strategy as to *what is important* also affects work. For example, health, safety, and overtime policies vary from one organization to the next and must be taken into account when you gather training content.

Business strategies affect what work is to be done, *how* the work is to be done, and *how well* the work is to be done.

Interviewing to Gather Relevant Content for Training

When gathering content for a task, ask yourself:
- *Are there any business strategies that affect how and how well the work is to be done?*

Roles and Responsibilities

Roles and responsibilities may be well defined for a discipline or position. All workers within that position have the same roles and responsibilities. Some organizations create job families where each worker may have slightly different roles and responsibilities (or jobs). Some organizations have clearly defined roles and responsibilities, others do not. When roles and responsibilities are not clear, you could inadvertently gather content that is outside the worker's usual roles and responsibilities. Doing so could lead to a dissatisfied customer.

When identifying relevant content, the SME may suggest that the roles and responsibilities should change and provide some logical rationale for making the change. For example, maintenance personnel may want operators to do more or less routine maintenance. Generally, the training you develop should focus on the *existing* roles and responsibilities of the target audience. If you change the roles and responsibilities or develop additional training without approval, the customer will be very dissatisfied. The customer does not want you to change the way it does business.

It is easy to develop additional training the customer does not want when two or more disciplines work together. For example, training is being developed for an operator who helps the maintenance person change components on large gas compressors. The operator is required to start and stop compressors and provide assistance to the mechanic.

The training for operators may explain the function of specific components, how they affect compressor operation, and how to adjust the components (if adjustable). For assisting maintenance in changing the components, the training may specify the operator's roles and responsibilities only, given the assumption that the operator has already received specialized training to start and stop the compressors. The training would not specify how to change components, which is not the operator's responsibility. Similarly, if training is being developed for the mechanic to change components, training would not include how to start and stop the compressor which is outside the mechanic's responsibilities.

A key question you can ask yourself is, *Is this training within the worker's roles and responsibilities?*

Hiring and Placement Qualifications

It is also important to know the organization's qualification policies for hiring and placement to determine the prerequisite skills of the target audience. It is not cost-effective or efficient to provide training when the target audience is already qualified to perform specific tasks. For example, if a journeyman is given reference resources and can do the work satisfactorily, then there is no need to develop training. Make sure the reference resources (e.g., equipment specifications manuals) are readily available. An important question you can ask the SME is, *If workers were given the information about..., could they do the work satisfactorily?*

Conversely, developing training at too high a level for workers new to the job can be very ineffective. For example, developing training that assumes that workers have the required mathematical skills when they do not can cause major difficulties for the trainee. Confirm with the SME the prerequisite skills workers must have to enter the job position.

Key questions you can ask yourself are:
- *Does the worker already know this because of his or her work experience, education, or prerequisite training?*
- *Can the worker complete the work satisfactorily by referring to other documents (e.g., the equipment specifications manual)?*

Key Factors for Problem Solving and Decision Making

The business model can also be used to identify factors that line workers may have to consider when solving problems and making decisions. In the following illustration, the constituents of the business model have been reorganized to show key factors for decision making. In the illustration, mission has not been shown because it is not necessary for many job-related decisions. If the mission was important, management and operational systems would reflect the mission.

TASKS
- conditions
- standards
- procedures
  – hazards
  – equipment
  – impact on PEMEO
  – alternative action

TECHNOLOGY AND PROCESS
- principles
- concepts
- components
- characteristics
- specifications and limitations
- process systems

DECISION MAKING
- reasons
- causes
- effects
- consequences

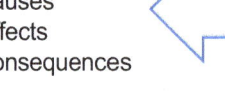

CORPORATE OBJECTIVES
- optimizing the operation
- minimizing losses
- minimizing costs
- maximizing profit
- ensuring employee and public safety
- protecting the environment
- adhering to legislation
- adhering to organizational policies
- ensuring a positive public image
- reinforcing a specific management style
- etc.

MANAGEMENT AND OPERATIONAL
- communication
- lines of authority
- limits of authority
- supervisor's expectations
- policies

Key questions you can ask yourself are:
- *What information does the worker need to make decisions in the best interest of the organization?*
- *Does this information help the worker make decisions?*

Section 2.7—*Reasons, Causes, Effects, and Consequences* provides further explanation on how the business constituents affect the work environment and potentially create problems to which workers must respond.

PART A Section 2
Using Critical Thinking Strategies to Identify Relevant Content

The business model helps you to understand the big picture so that you can ask quality questions to gather content that reflects the way the organization does business. For example, you are gathering content about *how* and *how well* to do a specific task. The business model identifies that corporate objectives, technology, and management and operational systems are directly related to the task. You can ask questions about how these constituents affect the *way* the task is performed and the *standards* of performance. Here are a few examples of questions you can ask about how constituents affect a task.

Corporate objectives—Are there any safety issues before, while, and after performing the task? Are there ways to do the task that cause the least stress to the equipment?

Technology—Are there ways to operate the technology that achieve optimal results? Does the technology limit the way the task is performed or the quality of results?

Management and Operational Systems—Are there any policies dictating how the task is to be performed? Are there any communication and documentation requirements? Do supervisors from different shifts and locations have different expectations on how and how well the task is to be performed? (For training purposes, there should be only one method for performing the task and all supervisors should have the same expectations for quality of results.)

The Exemplary Worker book *JobThink* uses the business model to provide a practical way for workers to understand their organizations so that they can effectively focus their efforts and make decisions in the best interests of their organizations. In the book, each constituent is explained and the interrelationships of the constituents are addressed. The use of resources and problem solving are also addressed. *JobThink* can help you ask quality questions that reflect the way the organization does business.

Interviewing to Gather Relevant Content for Training

LEARNING ACTIVITY 4

Use a business model

This learning activity helps you refine the questions you ask the SME to identify how the organizational constituents affect what work has to be done, how the work has to be done, and how well the work has to be done.

Identify an organization for which you develop training and reference resources.

The organization is: _____

1. The line of business is primarily:
    a. technical
    b. service

2. Referring to the list of generic corporate objectives in column one, list in order of priority the specific corporate objectives that apply to the organization you identified in question 1. Some of the corporate objectives in the list may not apply or you may want to add more objectives.

Generic Corporate Objectives	Organization-Specific Corporate Objectives
• safety	•
• environment	•
• legislation	•
• equipment reliability and life	•
• equipment optimization	•
• energy use	•
• quality	•
• loss control	•
• cost control	•
• customer satisfaction	•
• public image	•
• public disruption	•
• reputation	•
• communication	•
• teamwork	•
•	•
•	•

PART A Section 2
Using Critical Thinking Strategies to Identify Relevant Content

3. From business strategies and management and operational systems, policies and practices are created that dictate which tasks must be done, and how and how well the tasks must be done. Give three examples of polices and/or practices affecting how a task has to be performed.

   _____
   _____
   _____
   _____
   _____
   _____
   _____

4. How clearly are the roles and responsibilities of your training audience(s) defined?

   ☐ clearly defined

   ☐ not clearly defined

5. What could be the consequences if you inadvertently develop resources that change the roles and responsibilities of your training audience?

   _____
   _____
   _____
   _____

6. Identify the hiring qualifications of your training audience.

   Education: _____

   Job-specific training: _____

   Experience: _____

2.6 Work Effectively

The primary goals of training are to ensure workers can do their work safely, effectively, and efficiently and make decisions in their organization's best interests. Depending on the line of business, the content you gather may focus on performing tasks and/or on how things work. For a given job position, training is developed for tasks that have a significant contribution to achieving business goals and/or could create a loss if the tasks were performed poorly or not at all. When gathering content about how things work, you need to know the tasks so that the training content is relevant to the job position.

This section focuses on:
- determining the tasks for which you need to gather content
- defining the expectations for performing tasks:
  - what has to be done
  - how it has to be done
  - how well it has to be done

Workers can work more effectively when they clearly understand the expectations and are more likely to be motivated to achieve the desired results.

Determining tasks for training

Although an inventory of tasks can be made for a job position, training would not be developed for all the tasks. The following illustration shows the inventory of all possible tasks that fall within the worker's roles and responsibilities for a job position. Within this inventory:
- the **non-critical tasks (C)**. If the worker did not perform these tasks well, there would be minimal impact on the organization. Training would not be provided for these tasks.
- the **tasks for which training is now or will be provided (A)**. Some of these tasks are not considered critical but may indirectly impact corporate goals. Training includes generic knowledge and skills, such as basic training on using a control computer's display screens and keyboard, and generic safety training.

- the **critical tasks (B)**. These tasks are important to business success and may have the potential to create losses to PEMEO.
- the **critical tasks for which training must be provided (AB)**. Regulations may require that training and refresher training be provided for some of these tasks (e.g., pressure welding).

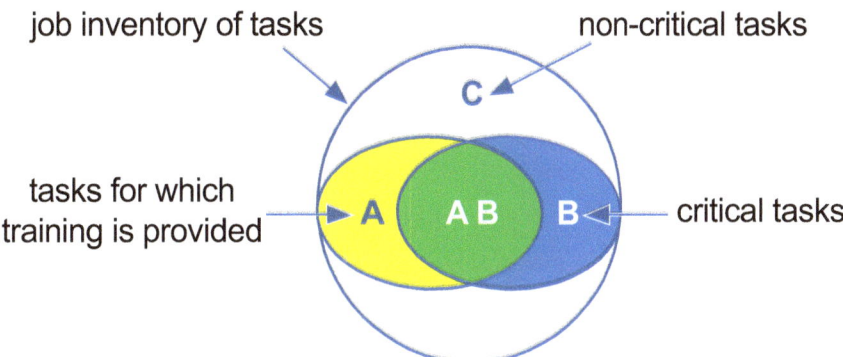

Often, standards and procedures are developed for critical tasks for which training would be provided. Support knowledge may also be provided so that the worker understands about the task before engaging in the work. This knowledge helps the worker to learn the task quickly, do the work effectively, and reduce the risk of losses.

Procedures and training are **not** required for non-critical tasks and some critical tasks if:
- The task is simple such as parking vehicles. If workers have the prerequisite skills to drive the vehicles and are given a parking plan, they can do the work.
- There is minimal risk to PEMEO if the workers make a mistake. For example, sending out a routine fax to multiple locations. For that particular application, if a destination was missed, little harm to PEMEO would be done. If the workers need help, assistance could be available.
- The task is very similar to another task that the worker can already do. The worker only needs to know the differences.
- Via the selection and promotion processes, the workers already have the skills and knowledge to do the work to the required standards if they are given the expectations and have access to task-specific information.

- The workers are only assisting another group.
- The task is performed infrequently.
- Close supervision is provided.
- The task is high risk, requires coordination among several workers, and is performed slightly differently every time.
- The task is performed by a competent specialist or contractor.

Procedures and training **are** required when:
- The worker does not have the specific skills and knowledge to carry out the task safely and effectively.
- The organization wants the task performed in a specific way.
- The task is complex.
- The task applies to a specific equipment model or site-specific technology.
- There are optimization opportunities.
- There is a risk of a negative impact on PEMEO.

When there is a risk of a negative impact on PEMEO, loss control measures (e.g., using fall arrest equipment) may be used to reduce the risk. The field of loss control is complex and involves all PEMEO domains. Some organizations have an entire department dedicated to loss control and risk management. Their objectives include managing business risk and being compliant with legislation. They may implement comprehensive loss control programs, especially for safety and the environment. Other departments such as finance, engineering, operations, and maintenance also have important responsibilities to control losses and manage risk.

While interviewing the SME, consider both optimization and loss control issues relating to PEMEO.

Always keep the constituents of the business model in mind when gathering content. By doing so, the content you gather for tasks will help workers:
- understand their organization's expectations for doing the tasks
- be more effective at performing the work
- be more effective at making decisions

When gathering content for tasks, you need to consider:
- what has to be done
- how it has to be done
- how well it has to be done

What has to be done

A critical part of working effectively and efficiently is to understand the expectations. Sometimes there are several similar tasks that have different applications and results. The task must be defined clearly to prevent misunderstandings. When gathering content, you can use several types of descriptor to define tasks so workers will know what has to be done.

Discipline, roles, and responsibilities

Worker qualifications or specialization may have to be stated because:
- only people with specific training and certification can do the work safely and effectively (e.g., pressure welder, electrician)
- the tasks are done differently depending on the specialization. For example:
  - Perform routine engine maintenance (operator)
  - Perform routine engine maintenance (mechanic)
  - Perform routine rectifier checks (operator)
  - Perform routine rectifier checks (electrician)

Action

Tasks are stated using verbs (such as *mix, start, adjust, enter*) to define the actions required to achieve the desired results.

Preconditions

Certain circumstances require that a task be performed. The word *when* may be used to state a precondition. For example:
- *When the customer asks for a rebate*, fill out the Customer Rebate form.
- *When the level in the tank reaches 85%*, start the discharge pump.

Conditions

Site conditions can dictate how a task has to be performed. If conditions change, the task may be performed differently or with a different level of skill:
- shut down the pump station *under normal conditions*
- locate pipe buried *beside metal buildings*
- dig trenches in *sandy soils*

Material

For some types of work (e.g., installation and repair), materials may be stated as part of the task descriptor. Different materials may require different tools and equipment and specific procedures for that material. For example:
- apply *two-component epoxy cement*
- install a *high-efficiency furnace*

Location

Where the task is performed can sometimes be very important. Doing the work at the wrong location could prove expensive. Sometimes the location can affect safety and make the task more difficult. If a person has to enter a confined space, such as a vessel, confined space entry procedures must be followed.

The location where the work is performed may require specific equipment. For example, driving to isolated areas may require that the vehicle be equipped with a radio. Some locations may have conditions that make work difficult. For example, the equipment and buildings may be very close together, making it necessary to work differently to access the work area with equipment and materials.

Standards of performance

Standards may be included in the task descriptor. Standards can affect how the work is done and the time it takes to do the work. More information on performance standards is provided in this section on *how well work has to be done.*

What cannot be used

Sometimes what cannot be used (e.g., tools or materials) or be done when performing the task must be stated. The

PART A Section 2
Using Critical Thinking Strategies to Identify Relevant Content

information may be part of the task descriptor or a separate statement. For example:
- without the use of power tools
- with materials that do **not** contain water-based glues

Critical thinking questions

Here are some critical thinking questions about *what has to be done*. Ask yourself these questions to determine the expectations for work and what you should include in the task descriptor. While you will not include all the answers to the questions in the task descriptor, you gain a better understanding of the task and of the relative content you must address.

Critical thinking questions you can ask are:
- *Who does the work?*
- *What has to be done?*
- *What created the need to do the task?*
- *What conditions affect doing the task?*
- *What materials are required?*
- *What tools and equipment are needed?*
- *Where is the task being done?*
- *When must the task be done?*

How it has to be done

There may be several different ways of performing the same task. You need to determine if the worker must follow a specific procedure or has freedom to decide how to do the work. When there is more than one way of doing the work, you need to get agreement as to the specific way the workers are going to be trained. After workers learn a specific way of working, they may be given the option to learn different or more advanced ways to work more effectively and efficiently.

Critical tasks must be performed in a specific way to ensure:
- no one gets hurt
- the environment is protected
- regulatory compliance
- equipment is used effectively and is not damaged
- materials are used effectively with minimal waste
- work is performed efficiently with minimal effort

- quality standards are met
- costs are controlled
- internal and external customers are satisfied

In the training, the reasons for performing a task in a specific way should be documented to give meaning to the work. When workers understand the reasons for doing work in a specific way, they are more motivated to do the work as expected. Understanding reasons also helps workers think through their work and respond more effectively when conditions change or something goes wrong.

Written procedures

For critical tasks, the organization may have written procedures, practices, or guidelines. If not, in consultation with the SME, you may have to gather the content and prepare a draft procedure.

NOTE You may have to write step-by-step procedures for tasks. Many organizations have specific formats. When developing a procedure, it is often possible to develop a comprehensive draft by interviewing the SME. However, for critical procedures, *a critical task analysis* should be done to identify safety and environmental issues and document controls to prevent incidents.

Many tasks can be divided into two to seven parts or major steps. A major step has a logical beginning and end and is a significant accomplishment towards completing the task. Here are two examples of dividing a task into major steps.

Replace a linoleum floor

Major step 1: Remove old linoleum.
Major step 2: Prepare floor.
Major step 3: Install new linoleum.

Start a pipeline pump station

Major step 1: Carry out pre-start checks.
Major step 2: Start booster pumps.
Major step 3: Start main pumps.

Major step 4: Increase throughput.
Major step 5: Monitor station operation.

Each major step is expanded to provide 5 to 9 specific action steps.

When gathering content for procedures, work with the SME to identify the major steps. Identifying the major steps helps the SME to organize his or her thoughts. Use the major steps as headings to structure the draft procedure.

When developing the action steps, some steps may have to be performed in a specific way to prevent losses to PEMEO and/or contribute to optimizing PEMEO. Ask yourself questions relating to LO-PEMEO and, if the questions seem relevant, ask the SME. For example:

What can go wrong if:
- *the step is performed poorly?*
- *the equipment does not respond as expected?*

When drafting the procedure, follow the format and style supplied by the customer. Make sure you put cautions and warnings **before** the action step. Check each step to ensure that it is not ambiguous. After you have drafted a procedure for a task, ask yourself:

How confident am I that, if the workers follow this procedure, they will work safely, effectively, and efficiently?

NOTE All procedures must be validated (verified) by the customer in the field to ensure they are correct. Validation should be carried out on the shop floor or in the field.

Section 4—*Relevant Content and Instructional Design* provides a strategy for gathering content to produce a draft procedure.

Specific policies and practices

Some organizations have specific policies and practices that must be applied to specific tasks. For example, the organization may have a policy that all customers must be treated courteously. The organization may also specify ways to be courteous. In the training, you may have to reinforce this policy and explain *why* it is important to business success.

Sequence of steps

The sequence of specific steps of a task may be important because of the need to contribute to corporate goals such as safety, preventing damage to equipment and materials, and working efficiently. An important question to ask yourself, and perhaps the SME, is, *Why are these step performed in this order?* Understanding the reasons motivates workers to perform the sequence correctly.

NOTE Many tasks can be performed by following step-by-step procedures. However, some tasks require the worker to have considerable knowledge to complete the task satisfactorily. For these types of task, it can be difficult to develop step-by-step procedures. A better approach is to develop a strategy for completing the task. In the training, provide the support knowledge to effectively apply the strategy.

Think ahead

Exemplary workers work safely, effectively, efficiently, and with the least effort. They think and plan ahead. Thoughtful arrangement of components, tools, and materials can contribute to working efficiently. There may be ways to reduce repetitive actions. There may be strategies to reduce walking distances. Some ways of carrying out specific actions can be more effective or less strenuous than others. Ask the SME for suggestions.

Communication

Effective communication is essential for effective coordination of work and to prevent harm to others. Communication with others may be required **before** doing the work, **during** work, and **after** the work is complete. Make a point of asking your SME about communication requirements.

Documentation

Documentation can be very useful and, in some cases, essential for carrying out the work. In the training resources, it may be necessary to identify where documentation is located. Some tasks also require documentation and distribution of the information. Unfortunately, for tasks where documentation of the work should be done, the documentation may be done incorrectly or not done. Include all documentation requirements in the training resources.

Critical thinking questions you can ask are:
- *Is there more than one way of performing the task?*
- *Why would one method be better than others?*
- *Why is this step of the procedure done this way?*
- *Is there a risk of people getting ill or injured?*
- *Can the environment be damaged?*
- *Can tools, equipment, and materials be damaged?*
- *How much waste is acceptable?*
- *Is there a need for communication and coordination?*
- *Is documentation required?*

WorkThink provides comprehensive information about how to work safely, effectively, and efficiently.

How well it has to be done

The purpose of performing tasks is to achieve specific results. Quality standards define how well the work has to be done and provides a means of performance assessment. When workers clearly understand how well the task is to be performed, they can focus their efforts to achieve the desired results (i.e., work effectively and efficiently). If workers are given feedback about the results of their work, they can adjust their performance if the results are not satisfactory. In some cases, the work may have to be redone.

Standards for tasks can apply to specific steps of a task, major steps of a task, and to the results. Standards can be expressed in terms of time, timeliness, quantity, and quality.

Interviewing to Gather Relevant Content for Training

Time may be an important factor to achieve specific results. Time can also be used to measure efficiency of work. For example:
- heat the materials at 300°C (570°F) for 30 minutes
- stir the mixture for 2 minutes
- it should take a maximum of 2 hours to do this task

Timeliness is about when some activity should start or be completed. Coordination and sequence of activities may also be important. For example:
- the materials must be delivered by 10:00 a.m.
- the area must be cleaned up immediately after the installation is complete
- the process must be shut down and isolated by 2:00 a.m.

Quantity can be measured in terms of amount and rate. For example:
- add 2 litres (0.5 gallons) of water
- set the delivery at 50 cubic metres/hour (315 barrels/hour)
- make 20 couplings/hour

Quality can be difficult to describe for some types of work. Often, quality involves the degree of precision, accuracy, or tolerance. Sometimes quality standards for work include measurements of time, timeliness, and quantity (e.g., rates). Examples where measurement units are used to specify quality are:
- machine the parts to within ± 0.025 mm (1/1000 in.)
- use an air hose that is rated for at least 500 kPa (80 psi)
- set the product mix to 70% A and 30% B
- ensure the water content is less than 0.5%

Knowing the standards for *how* and *how well* a task must be done provides workers with the incentive for meeting the standards. When workers know the expectations, they are most likely to work towards achieving those expectations. In addition to organizational standards for performance appraisal and policies, there are many other sources of standards such as:
- ISO 9000 (quality)
- ISO 14000 (environment)
- regulated standards (boiler and pressure vessel, welding,

electrical, hoisting, fire detection and suppression, occupational health and safety)
- engineering codes and standards
- customer specifications

Some tasks, such as monitoring and conducting pre-start checks, do not have standards that are practical for determining satisfactory performance. The worker does the tasks satisfactorily by following each step of a procedure or checklist. In the training resources you develop, you could state that the standard is to perform the task in accordance with the steps of the procedure.

Indicators of performance are sometimes used as a practical way of assessing performance. For example, maintenance records may indicate whether a truck driver is operating the truck in ways that minimize wear and tear. Maintenance records for the truck can be compared to the maintenance records of other trucks in the fleet. Significant differences indicate the amount of care for the truck.

Performance indicators are also a practical way for workers to determine whether they have satisfactorily performed specific steps of a task. In some of the training content you gather, you may find it beneficial to document indicators of performance so that the workers have a way to assess their own performance.

Ease of doing work
"Many jobs are easy to do, the hard part is learning to do the job."

When gathering content, keep in mind that the resources you will develop contribute to the ease of learning and help workers learn to do their jobs effectively and efficiently.

Management can set goals, but workers play an important part in ensuring the goals are met. When interviewing SMEs, keep in mind that one of your responsibilities is to develop training resources that help workers do the work to their organization's satisfaction.

Critical thinking questions you can ask are:
- *How well am I to do the task?*
- *How do I know that I have done the task satisfactorily?*

- *How do I know that I have done a major step satisfactorily?*
- *How do I know that I have completed this step satisfactorily?*

WorkThink explains performance standards and the challenges of establishing standards in more detail.

Work effectively

This learning activity helps you refine the questions you ask the SME to define tasks clearly.

1. Give three reasons why training is not developed for all tasks that fall within a person's roles and responsibilities (i.e., inventory of tasks).

   _____
   _____
   _____

2. Give three reasons why training is developed for specific tasks that fall within a person's roles and responsibilities (i.e., inventory of tasks).

   _____
   _____
   _____

3. Identify a task performed in your workplace or home. Use the following table of descriptors to ensure that the task is stated clearly. For most tasks, not all of the descriptors are required to ensure that you (or others) clearly understand what has to be done.

Task Descriptors	
discipline	materials
action	tools and equipment
preconditions	location
conditions	standards of performance

PART A Section 2
Using Critical Thinking Strategies to Identify Relevant Content

Example:
The task is: <u>Re-energize high-voltage breakers</u>

The task is: When a maintenance task is complete and all locks have been removed, the electrician re-energizes the high-voltage breaker in the motor control center (MCC). The electrician must wear the specified arc flash PPE and follow the written procedure for re-energizing breakers.

The task is: _____

Statement of the task: _____

_____

_____

_____

4. Most tasks have several major activities or steps. Select a task and list the major steps in proper sequence. Your task may have less than five major steps.

   The task is: _____
   Major Step 1: _____
   Major Step 2: _____
   Major Step 3: _____
   Major Step 4: _____
   Major Step 5: _____

5. For many tasks, there are critical action steps that must be performed in a specific way to prevent losses to PEMEO and/or contribute to optimizing PEMEO. Using the task you identified in question 4, identify two action steps that affect PEMEO.

   Optimize PEMEO

   Action step: _____

   When performing the step, what contributes to optimizing PEMEO? _____

   _____

47

Loss to PEMEO

Action step: _____

When performing the step, what could cause a loss to PEMEO? _____

_____

6. What communication is required before, during, or after the task is performed?

   _____

   _____

7. Using the task identified in question 3, state the standard(s) for satisfactory performance. Consider time, timeliness, quality, and quantity when specifying the standards of performance.

   Standard(s) of performance: _____

   _____

   _____

2.7 Reasons, Causes, Effects, and Consequences

One of the main reasons exemplary workers are effective at their jobs is that they continually determine reasons, causes, and consequences before, during, and after completing work. With the understanding that they gain, they can make *good* decisions and take actions that contribute to business success and minimize losses.

You need to apply the same thinking strategies when gathering content and developing resources so that the training contributes to improved employee, job, and corporate performance. Workers (i.e., the learners) are more motivated to learn when they are given practical reasons for acquiring the knowledge and performing the tasks well. Training takes on meaning when workers know the reasons, causes, effects, and consequences relating to the tasks and technology.

Often the content you gather relates directly to the workplace. To gather useful content and write training resources that focus on improving performance, you need to understand the relevant reasons, causes, effects, and consequences that relate to the topic. Because the SME may not volunteer this information, you need to ask quality questions to draw out the required information. However, you may not have enough knowledge about the topic to know what questions to ask. You need a strategy to determine the types of question that are important to the job and organization. This section describes the interrelationships between reasons, causes, effects, and consequences. Criteria for asking quality questions relating to these concepts are also given to help you focus your thinking to determine which questions to ask.

> **NOTE**
>
> The terms *reason* and *cause* are often used as synonyms. However, in this book, these terms have different meanings.
>
> **Reasons** relate to: rationale, motive, goal, purpose, intent, and by design. In organizations, reasons provide the rationale for the workplace environment.
>
> **Causes** relate to: failure, unintended happenings, and unpredicted events. In business and work environments, causes often result in negative consequences.

The concepts and thinking strategies associated with reasons, causes, effects, and consequences are complex. This section provides a brief description of the concepts and related thinking strategies. Refer to *MetaThink* for a comprehensive description.

The following illustration provides an overview of the relationships between reasons, causes, effects, and consequences.

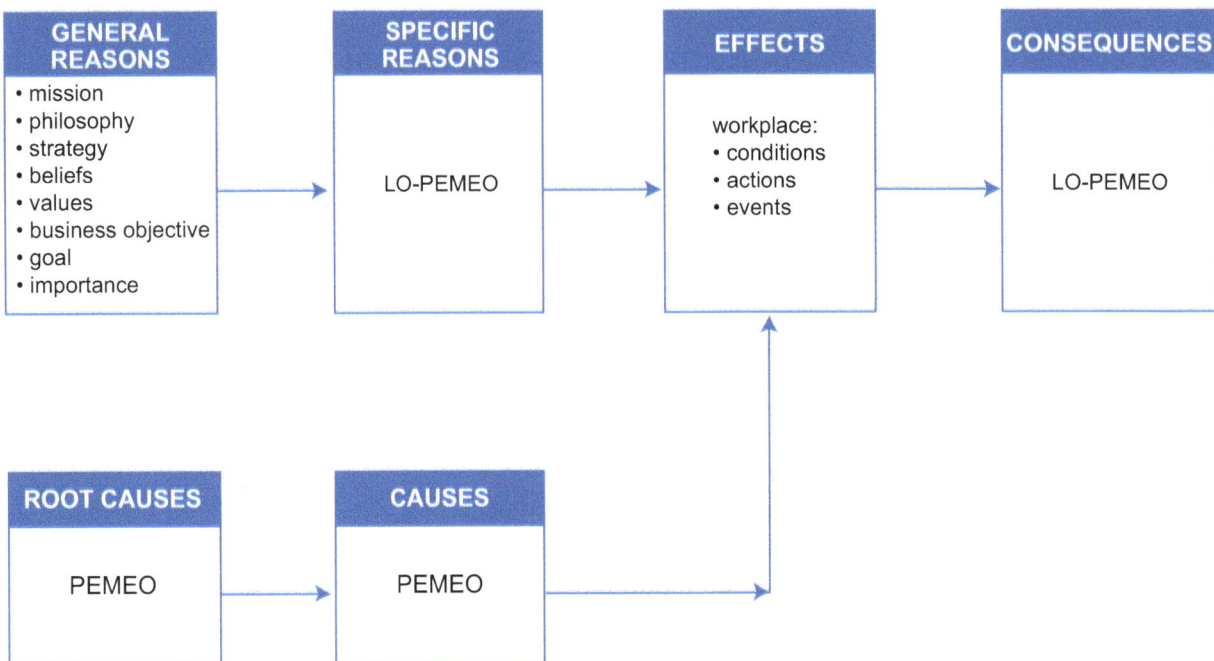

Workplace environments are complex. Equipment, materials, people, policies, practices, business strategies, management styles, supervision, tasks, and employee attitudes all contribute to the workplace environment. You need to understand the reasons the workplace is the way it is (i.e., effect) to be able to gather content and develop training materials that reflect the organization.

Reasons and effects

When gathering content, you should record the associated reasons to give meaning to the content. To determine the reasons a workplace is the way it is and the reasons people work the way they do, you need to ask *Why...?* about the work environment (effect). You could consider a very broad set of reasons for which you could ask *Why...?* questions, making the interviewing process difficult and inefficient. Fortunately, there are specific types of reason that are important to organizations. To be able to ask relevant *why* questions, you need a basic understanding of organizations.

The business model explained in Section 2.5—*Use a Business Model* provides a useful way to identify organizational issues affecting exemplary job performance. Some key points are taken from the model to explain **organizational design** in a way that helps you determine relevant reasons and effects.

An organization is created by design. Its fundamental identity is defined by terms such as the following:

GENERAL REASONS
• mission • philosophy • strategy • beliefs • values • business objective • goal • importance

To function, the organization must have money, equipment, materials, and people. To ensure activities are conducted in ways that support its mission, philosophy, strategies, and goals, management provides direction to employees by:
- identifying the work and tasks that must be carried out
- defining roles and responsibilities
- establishing management and administration to coordinate work
- developing policies, practices, procedures, and standards

All of the above items can be classified according to PEMEO. The **reasons** for the way the organization is designed are to prevent losses and optimize the use of resources, including people (i.e., LO-PEMEO).

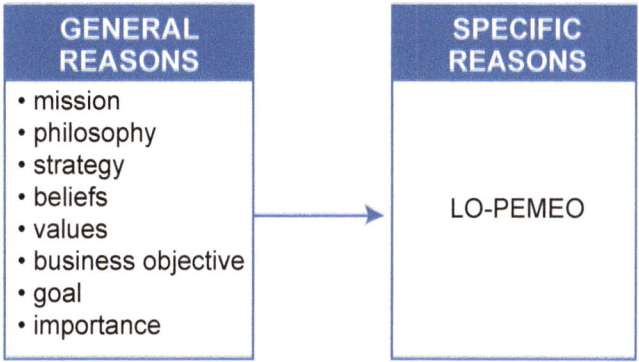

For example, if upper management believes that safety is important, then policies, practices, procedures, equipment, supervision, and training reflect that commitment to safety.

The **effect** of an organization addressing all the domains of PEMEO is the creation of the work environment. Conditions, actions, and events associated with PEMEO define that work environment and the dynamics that are taking place to achieve production goals.

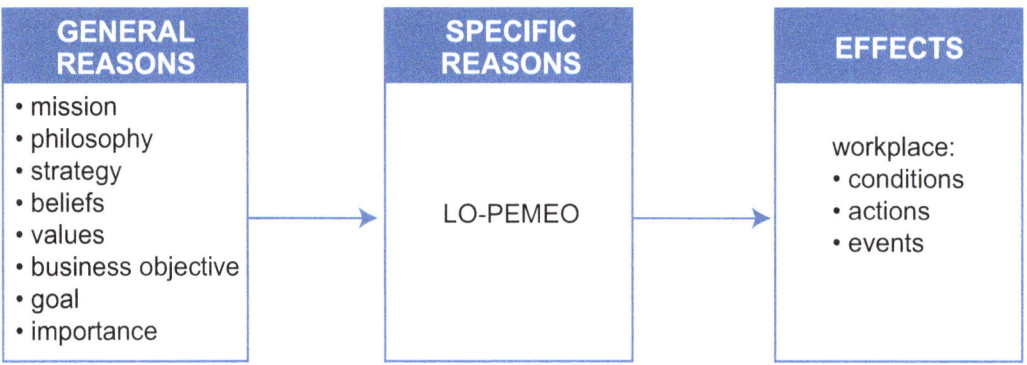

The results of production are a set of negative and positive **consequences** (LO). The consequences most important to an organization are those that affect PEMEO. For the organization, the most positive consequence is that production contributes to its mission and does so in a way that supports its beliefs and values. Unfortunately, negative consequences can also occur, such as workplace injuries or equipment failure. Consequences and their link to effect (i.e., the workplace) are explained in more detail in the next subsection.

Often the content you gather relates directly to the workplace. To determine the reasons why the work environment is the way it is and why the people work the way they do, you need to reverse the above thinking process by asking *Why...?* questions about the effect (conditions, actions, and events). Often you can determine the immediate reason for an effect by examining one or more domains of PEMEO. A more general reason can often be identified by asking the *reason for the reason* (i.e., *why for the why*) For example, a compressor's suction pressure is set at the maximum recommended limit. The reason for the high suction pressure is to maximize throughput. The reason the throughput is maximized may be to maximize revenue or meet customer orders. Often the reason for the reason will be an organization's mission, philosophy, belief, value, strategy, or business goal.

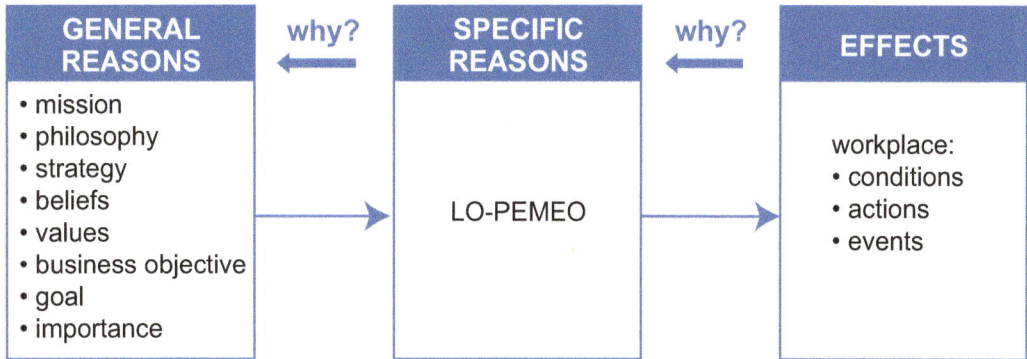

Effect (workplace conditions, actions, and events), Reasons (LO-PEMEO) and Reasons for Reasons (beliefs, etc.)

In industrial settings, the reasons often relate to the equipment itself or to the materials that are being manufactured, changed, or monitored. Equipment operation can be explained in terms of scientific concepts or engineering design principles. The explanation uses variables such as temperature, pressure, and force to describe how and why equipment works in a particular way and why the variables (and their setpoints or operating ranges) are important for safe, effective, and efficient equipment operation and product quality.

NOTE The concept of variables can be applied in many ways. For example, variables can be the number of customers, weather, and types of material. Using variables as a thought process can help you ask more comprehensive questions when interviewing the SME to gain a fuller understanding of the issues affecting the workers. The variables that can change or be changed are especially important.

When workers know the reasons for performing specific tasks, they can direct their efforts more effectively. When they know the reasons for performing some steps in a specific way, they are likely to be more conscientious when carrying out the steps.

Interviewing to Gather Relevant Content for Training

During the interview with the SME, you can ask questions to determine *why* a certain variable is important (i.e., the reason). For example:
- *Why is this task important?*
- *Why are the steps to a task performed in this order?*
- *Why must these steps be performed in a specific way?*
- *Why are these specific safety precautions taken?*
- *Why did the event occur?*
- *Why does the internal customer require this work assignment to be completed on schedule?*
- *Why is this variable important for product quality?*
- *Why must this equipment be operated at this setpoint or within this range?*

The types of *why* question you can ask to determine reasons are often about workplace conditions, actions, and events that relate to PEMEO.

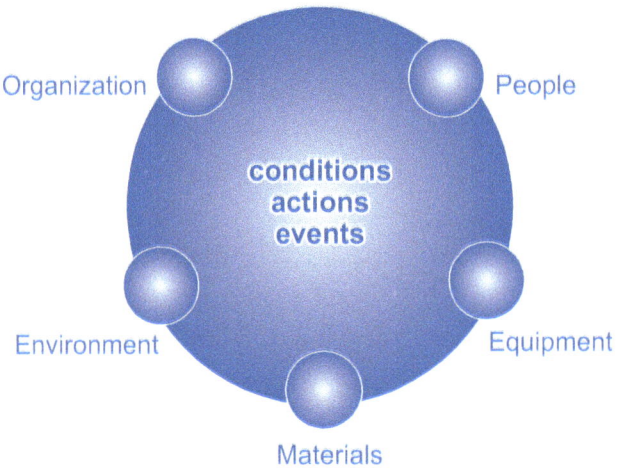

PEMEO are the reasons for the Workplace Environment (Conditions, Actions, and Events)

Often, training materials describe the purpose and importance of tasks and technology:
- the purpose of tasks is to achieve desired results
- the purpose of technology is defined by its function

To determine the *importance* of a task or technology, ask why it is important to workers, the job, and the corporation. The answers will relate to one or more PEMEO domains.

Effects and consequences

In addition to determining *reasons* for a specific variable (effects—condition, action, or event), examine the *consequences* of the variable. Here are some considerations relative to consequences:

- Of all possible consequences, those affecting PEMEO are the most important to organizations.
- A condition, employee action, or event impacting one PEMEO domain most likely impacts other PEMEO domains (see Section 2.2—*Preventing Illness and Injury (safety)*).
- If a job variable changes, consequences can also change (e.g., the supplied materials are contaminated with a toxic substance).
- The worker must know the consequences for PEMEO if a variable changes or does not change when it is supposed to.
- Over time, variables can slowly change and the worker must compensate by making incremental changes to the way he or she performs the work (e.g., as an engine wears, its power may decrease).
- The worker may be required to document the effects, consequences, reasons, and response.

The purpose for operating equipment and for workers to do work is to achieve specific results or outcomes. However, the actual results or outcomes may be different than expected. Conditions such as seasonal temperatures or material quality can affect the results. The consequences of an event can be positive or negative depending on the circumstances. Results and outcomes are all consequences of specific conditions, actions, or events.

It may be useful to include content that helps the worker predict consequences and take the appropriate action to achieve desired results and minimize loss. Predicting consequences can be difficult because a change in conditions, actions, or events can produce a different set of consequences. Workers must continually predict consequences that have a significant impact on the corporation, the job, and employees. In some cases, in the training resources, you will need to identify loss control measures to reduce potential losses.

There are many possible consequences for a given situation, depending on who or what the consequences affect. For businesses, the most important consequences are those that impact PEMEO and corporate goals.

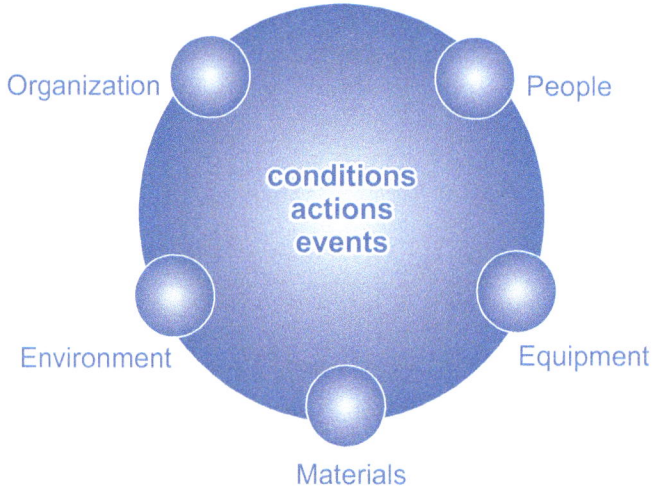

Conditions, Actions, and Events Impact PEMEO

When workers understand the consequences for a given condition, action, or event, they can often find ways to optimize the use of assets and reduce the risk of losses.

Reasons can explain normal work practices which lead to desirable consequences, especially optimization of assets and the minimization of losses. However, if a job variable changes, consequences can also change. Or, if a job variable does not change when it is supposed to, the desired result (consequence) may not be achieved.

Causes, effects, and consequences

Unintended and unpredictable workplace conditions, actions, or events (i.e., effect) can create serious consequences for PEMEO. Often an unintended event is the result of a sequence of **causes** and effects. For example:
- a natural gas line had a flaw (root cause)
- the flaw caused the line to rupture
- the escaping gas *caused* a fire (event)
- the fire *caused* the building to burn down (consequence)
- the employees are out of work (consequence)

The initiating cause is often identified as the root cause. In the previous example, the gas line flaw is the root cause and the consequence is that employees are out of work. The root cause must be corrected to prevent the event from reoccurring.

Generally, one or more domains of PEMEO are the cause of the event and resulting consequences.

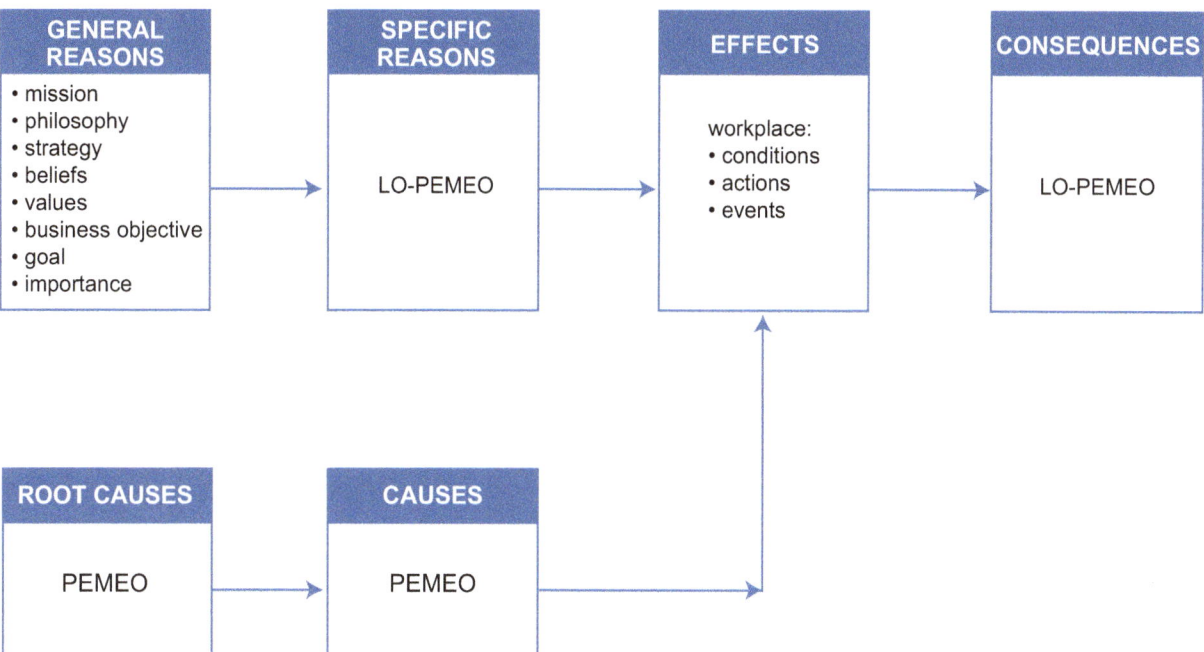

As shown in the above diagram, reasons, causes, effects, and consequences are closely related, PEMEO being the most common thread.

When you think there may be potentially negative consequences to PEMEO, you need to ask the SME *Why...?* questions to determine the causes. When possible, identify the root cause because correcting the immediate cause may not provide a long-term solution.

For the most common abnormal operating conditions, you may have to identify and document the causes, indicators of a problem, and worker responses. It may be useful to provide a troubleshooting chart when there may be more than one cause for a problem or multiple problems with equipment operation. Consider creating a three to five column chart

Interviewing to Gather Relevant Content for Training

for troubleshooting such as the following example about a barbecue. Note that the titles may change for any given customer or application.

Condition	Possible Causes	Diagnosis	Corrective Action	Indication of Correction
1. barbecue does not light	• electric igniter does not work	• does igniter spark?	• clean and adjust igniter	• spark observed
	• propane not getting to burner	• is propane bottle valve open? • is safety valve on propane bottle open?	• turn valve to fully open • close propane valve fully and then fully open	• propane can be heard going to burner • propane can be heard going to burner
2. cooks unevenly	• •	• •	• •	• •

When interviewing the SME, ask *What if...?* questions about variables to link cause to effect. Determine the potential consequences and identify the first response. Section 2.8—*What if...? Questions* describes a structured thinking strategy for asking *What if...?* questions.

Linking Reasons, Causes, Effects, and Consequences

The following diagram shows the interrelationships between reasons, causes, effects, and consequences.

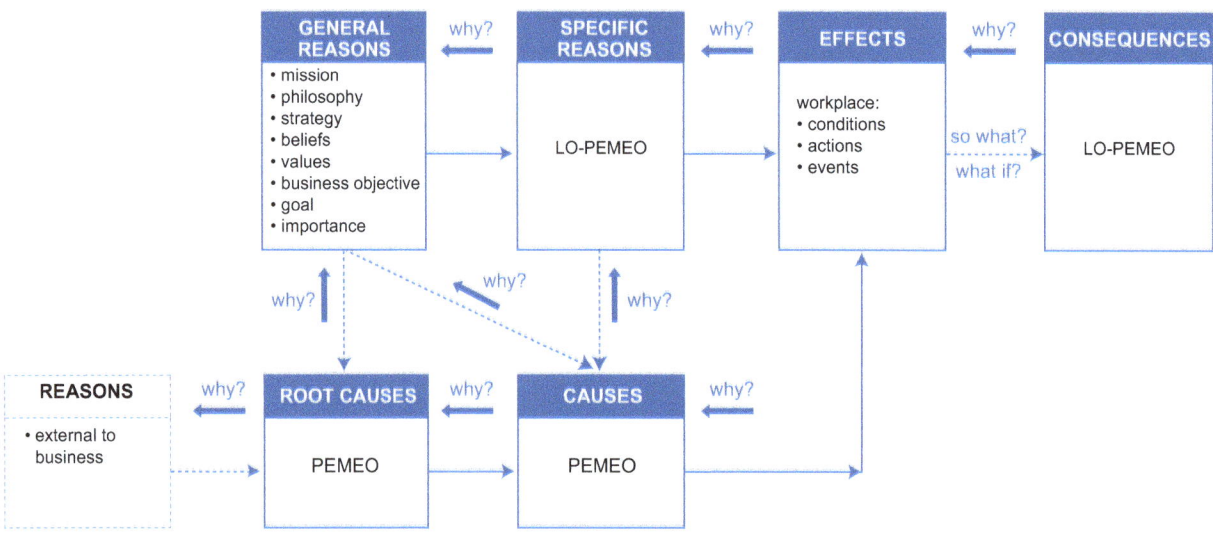

Interrelationship between Reasons, Causes, Effects, and Consequences

Start with an existing situation (effects) and ask *Why...?* to identify the reasons or causes for the situation. If you know the consequences, you can determine the causes or reasons by first examining the conditions, actions, or events in the workplace (i.e., the effects that originated from the reasons and causes).

The type of *Why...?* questions to ask and the answers to the questions relate to PEMEO because PEMEO is the most common thread within the organization and work environment. Start by examining the conditions, actions, and events in the work environment. Use the variables that are described in the previous section of this book. The variables give you direction for asking meaningful questions. The answers to the questions give meaning to why the variables are important to the organization, the job, and employees.

IMPORTANT

When gathering content about equipment variables, identify the variables that can change and determine the:
- reasons the variables are at a specific setpoint or within a specific operating range
- causes for the variables to shift
- consequences if the variables shift from setpoint or outside the operating range
- indicators that the variables have shifted
- first response to the abnormal condition

Reasons, causes, effects, consequences

Workers can be more effective in directing their efforts to achieve satisfactory results when they know the reasons, causes, effects, and consequences for doing the work and why the work processes and conditions are the way they are. This learning activity helps you refine the questions you ask the SME to identify reasons, causes, effects, and consequences relevant to the specific work and technical processes.

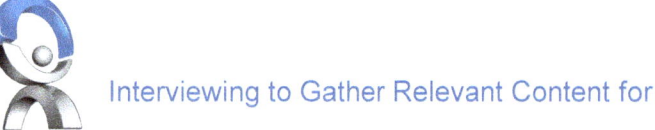

Interviewing to Gather Relevant Content for Training

1. Identify an equipment variable. What is the reason for the variable to be operated at setpoint or within a specific range?

   _____
   _____

2. Identify an incident (e.g., equipment failure) that had a negative effect in the workplace. What was the *cause* for the incident?

   _____
   _____

3. Using the incident identified in question 2, specify the *consequences* for PEMEO.

   _____
   _____

2.8 *What if...?* Questions

For workers to be effective in performing tasks and making decisions, they must predict the potential consequences should variables change or something goes wrong. Identifying *what can go wrong* can be very difficult because the question is too broad—it can be very difficult to know what questions to ask. To focus their thinking, exemplary workers consider what can go wrong with PEMEO by asking *What if...?* questions about conditions, actions, and events that could occur and cause PEMEO to function poorly, behave abnormally, or fail. If there is a concern, they determine the immediate effect. If there is a potential for loss, they take action to reduce the potential of an incident occurring and/or the severity of the consequences.

You can apply the same thinking strategy to identify relevant content about things that can go wrong. Your SME can supply the answers.

PART A Section 2
Using Critical Thinking Strategies to Identify Relevant Content

NOTE

SafeThink uses a structured thinking strategy to ask *What if...?* questions to identify the immediate effect and potential consequences that affect people's safety. Here, we ask *What if...?* questions to determine the immediate effect and potential consequences for all domains of PEMEO.

The following table provides some examples of *What if...?* questions to determine the consequences.

What can go wrong with PEMEO?		
Domain	***What if...?*** *(conditions, actions, events)*	**Immediate Effect**
People	• What if I put the crates in the alley?	• Workers on the other side would have their escape route blocked.
	• What if I don't close the valve fully?	• Toxic gas will leak to the atmosphere.
	• What if I suffer fatigue because I have worked long hours to complete a job?	• My ability to think through the work and concentrate is diminished.
Equipment	• What if the conveyor starts suddenly?	• My arm would be caught in the drive chain.
	• What if the clamp on the winch line breaks?	• The load will fall to the ground and the cable will snake through the air.
	• What if the equipment is put on computer control?	• The equipment will start and stop without warning.
Materials	• What if high-grade steel sockets are replaced with low-grade steel sockets?	• The sockets could break when the usual force is applied.
	• What if the materials can easily disintegrate?	• Dust will contaminate the atmosphere.
	• What if the wood pry lever breaks?	• I will fall backwards. • The wood will split into two long sharp points.

(continued)

What can go wrong with PEMEO?		
Domain	*What if...?* (conditions, actions, events)	**Immediate Effect**
Environment	• What if mice invade the storage area?	• Shelves and supplies will be covered with infectious droppings.
	• What if the number of workers on site increases four-fold?	• The variety and dynamics of work would increase dramatically.
	• What if I step out of the vehicle onto icy pavement?	• I could slip.
Organization	• What if the renovators are painting?	• The vapors could get into the ventilation system and travel to other parts of the building.
	• What if the supplier replaces neoprene gloves with rubber gloves?	• The solvent will rapidly penetrate the gloves and contact the skin.
	• What if the crew is short staffed?	• Completion of the job activities on time will be difficult.

You may have difficulties asking quality *What if...?* questions that apply to the Organization domain. Here are some examples of conditions, actions, and events related to the Organization domain that can affect PEMEO. To familiarize yourself with the list, check off the examples that most likely apply to your SME's organization.

☐ poor scheduling (timing of activities)

☐ not following coordination plans

☐ change in the work process

☐ shortage of staff

☐ lack of competent workers assigned to a specific task

☐ policy that can cause harm under certain conditions (e.g., wearing PPE in extremely hot environments can lead to heat stroke if rest periods are not taken frequently)

PART A Section 2
Using Critical Thinking Strategies to Identify Relevant Content

- ☐ work group introduces new hazard
- ☐ third party fails to maintain equipment/facilities
- ☐ supplier changes standards or composition of components or materials
- ☐ unpredicted large customer order
- ☐ cancellation or delay of large customer order (e.g., may have excessive inventory on site)
- ☐ failure to communicate priorities
- ☐ lack of documentation
- ☐ roles and responsibilities for work assignment not clear
- ☐ administrative process inadequate for maintaining inventory
- ☐ failure to carry out routine safety inspections
- ☐ failure to follow up/correct identified safety deficiencies

The table *What can go wrong with PEMEO?* lists some immediate effects of conditions, actions, or events associated with PEMEO. The immediate effect may not have an impact (consequence) on PEMEO. However, the consequence of the effect may affect one or more domains of PEMEO. For example, if a surface is slippery and the effect is that someone falls, the fall itself does not affect the person—however, that person's reaction and the impact due to the fall can have a variety of consequences, depending on the conditions:

- the surface may be flat
- the surface may be cluttered with sharp, jagged objects
- the fall may be into a vat or lagoon
- the fall may be into moving equipment components
- the fall could be in the path of moving equipment
- the person falling could be carrying materials or equipment that can get damaged
- the person falling could get injured by the objects being carried
- if another person is nearby, that person could get hit by the one who is falling or by the objects he or she is carrying
- the person falling can react in an attempt to recover from the fall and strain back muscles

Interviewing to Gather Relevant Content for Training

When asking *What if...?* questions, first determine the immediate effects. Then ask yourself if the immediate effects can have or lead to consequences for PEMEO.

What if...? questions are about conditions, actions, and events and most often about changes in conditions, actions and events. Changes can often be defined in terms of variables.

For variables that can affect the worker, other people, the job, or the organization, ask yourself what is normal or ideal, and then ask yourself how a change in variables can have negative consequences for PEMEO. For example, regarding equipment, ask, *What if... (the variables are not within specifications or do not behave as expected)... what are the consequences for PEMEO?* If you think the consequences are significant, ask the SME if the change is a concern and how the worker should respond to the situation. You may have to work with the SME to determine the worker's response by determining the reasons or causes for the change and by determining the lines and limits of authority for the job position.

Workers may have to respond immediately to abnormal/emergency conditions or events to minimize the severity of the consequences. Your customer may have an emergency response plan which requires workers from different disciplines to carry out specific actions. If your customer has an emergency response plan, you may have to make reference to it in the training material you develop.

While interviewing the SME, ask yourself *What if...?* questions to determine what can go wrong and the possible immediate effects. Then ask yourself these questions:
- *Could the worker or others become ill and/or injured?*
- *Could the environment or public be affected?*
- *Could property, equipment, or materials be damaged?*
- *What should be the worker's first response if an incident occurs?*
- *What could the worker do to minimize the possibility of an incident occurring and/or the potential severity of the consequences?*

If the questions seem relevant, ask the SME for answers.

For many of the incidents identified by the *What if...?* questions, workers will be more effective in responding to the incidents by:
- determining in advance the response they would make
- rehearsing their responses in their minds by imagining how they would respond to the incident. Rehearsing increases the possibility that they will respond immediately and effectively.

To help workers identify potential incidents and respond effectively should an incident occur, you may consider:
- documenting the potential for incidents and the required first responses
- providing exercises to reinforce their learning
- assessing their knowledge

Ask yourself the following questions about variables:
- *Which variables are important to the job?*
- *Why are the variables important? (reason)*
- *What are the desired specifications for the variables?*
- *Which variables can be controlled?*
- *Which variables can change?*
- *Why does a variable change? (reason or cause)*
- *What if PEMEO domains do not perform as expected—what are the immediate effects?*
- *What are the indicators that a variable has changed?*
- *What happens when a variable changes? (consequences for PEMEO)*
- *What must be done in response to a change in a variable? (reasons, limits of authority)*
- *How do work processes (operations and maintenance) affect the variables? (consequences for PEMEO)*
- *What are the worker's roles and responsibilities if the consequences for PEMEO are immediate and severe (i.e., the desired response to an abnormal or emergency situation)?*

Answers to these types of questions give you a more complete understanding of variables affecting the worker's job. With

Interviewing to Gather Relevant Content for Training

this knowledge, you reduce the number of questions you need to continually ask yourself or the SME so that the interviewing process is efficient.

What if . . . ? questions

This learning activity helps you refine your skills to ask the SME *What if...?* questions to determine what can go wrong.

Fill out the following table. Think of a specific task or technical process and ask *What if...?* questions about PEMEO. Consider all domains of PEMEO when determining the immediate effect.

What can go wrong with PEMEO?		
Domain	**What if...?** (conditions, actions, events)	**Immediate Effect**
People	•	•
	•	•
	•	•
Equipment	•	•
	•	•
	•	•
Materials	•	•
	•	•
	•	• •

(continued)

What can go wrong with PEMEO?		
Domain	What if...? (conditions, actions, events)	Immediate Effect
Environment	•	•
	•	•
	•	•
Organization	•	•
	•	•
	•	•

2.9 View Issues from Other People's Perspectives

A useful strategy to identify relevant content is to imagine being the:
- trainee receiving the training
- the coach or trainer delivering the training
- the supervisor or team leader concerned about employee, job, and corporate performance

To successfully view issues from a different person's perspective, pretend to be that person with his or her education, experiences, skills, beliefs, values, and personal attributes. The saying, *You have to walk a mile in the other person's shoes to understand their situation.* has a lot of merit but may not be sufficient to understand that person's concerns and issues and can be cause for misunderstandings. Your experiences, skills, and abilities may be different from that person's. That person may be more or less capable than you in dealing with the situation. Ask yourself, *If I were that person, how would I view the issue?*

While interviewing the SME, the most important point of view is that of the worker who must learn to perform the work satisfactorily. Imagine being a person starting a new job or new position. A person beginning work in a new job position has many immediate concerns and questions, including:

Questions	Regarding
• What am I supposed to do? Not do?	– tasks
• How am I supposed to do it?	– procedures
• How well am I supposed to do it?	– expectations & standards
• What can go wrong?	– impact on PEMEO
• What should I do if something goes wrong?	– limits and lines of authority
• What is important?	– to the job and the business
• What are my roles and responsibilities?	– in this job position
• What policies affect me and my work?	– to comply with this organization's way of doing business

Workers starting a new position may not be given the answers to these types of question which can be stressful. Over time, the workers will discover the answers for themselves, provided they know what to ask. One of the goals of a training program is to get workers productive in the least amount of time. Why not give the answers to these questions in the documentation and through the training administration system? Let the documentation and training system be one way to provide direction, improve efficiencies in learning the job, and reduce worker stress.

As the worker gains experience in a job position, he or she may have more complex concerns and questions:

PART A Section 2
Using Critical Thinking Strategies to Identify Relevant Content

Questions
- How does it work?
- What is the reason?
- How does my work affect other jobs?
- What would happen if . . . ?
- What is the best response to the problem?
- What caused the problem?
- What is the best long-term solution?
- How can I prevent . . . ?
- Is there an easier or more efficient way?

Regarding
– technology and processes
– for events to occur
– and impact on business performance
– changes were made
– in the interest of business

– resulting in a loss to PEMEO
– for the business

– downgrading events
– of working

In the following illustration, the worker is asking questions related to the job. The worker needs answers to these types of question to perform effectively.

> What's important to the business?
> What does the team leader expect of me?
> What am I supposed to do?
> How am I supposed to do it?
> How do I know I've done well?
> How does my work affect others?
> Is there a better way?
> What tools and equipment are used?

> Could I get hurt?
> Could I injure others?
> Could I damage the equipment?
> Does this product affect the environment?
> How much waste is acceptable?
> How can I prevent...?
> Will the customer be satisfied?
> What should I do if ...?

> What would happen if ...?
> Do I have the authority to take action?
> What action?
> Whom should I inform?
> What does ...?
> How does ...?
> What caused ...?
> What is the reason?
> What are the consequences for ...?

> What questions should I be asking?
> What answers do I need?

When imagining you are the trainee, experience the content that you are gathering to determine if it makes sense or provides adequate directions. Ask yourself, *Is this content detailed enough to help trainees understand and do their jobs?*

Sometimes you may have difficulties in getting the SME to agree to the detail you want to include in the content to help trainees learn effectively. SMEs may forget what it was like learning the content in the first place. Over time, experienced people tend to generalize information to make their work easier. Unfortunately, they may also have forgotten some of the detail. Some SMEs are very quick learners and do not appreciate the difficulties others may have in learning their jobs. Explain to the SME that, considering the trainees' entry knowledge and skills, it is important to make sure that the content is well explained so that learning is effective.

While interviewing the SME, keep in mind that you have a mandate to produce training and reference resources. There may be opportunities to consider how you will present the content in a way that best helps the trainee learn. Imagine being the trainer. *Have you considered the safety issues before, while, and after providing training?* Imagine observing the trainee's reaction to the instruction. *Do you think that the trainee, with his or her experiences and abilities, will understand?* If you have concerns about the best way to present the content, you may consider asking the SME how he or she has provided that part of the instruction. If SMEs have a training role, they may have gained insights into ways to present the training effectively.

Supervisors and team leaders represent the organization and are expected to reflect organizational values, reinforce policies, and work towards achieving business goals and specific results. They also want workers new to the job to be safe and to learn to perform effectively. Always keep in mind the supervisor's concerns (especially the corporate objectives) so that the content has value for the worker, the job, and the organization. After all, the supervisor may be the person who approves your work.

PART A   Section 2
Using Critical Thinking Strategies to Identify Relevant Content

Viewing issues from other people's perspectives

This learning activity helps you refine your skills to determine other people's perspectives so that the content you gather from the SME takes into account the impact of your audience's job on other jobs and vice versa.

State what would be important to and what would be an issue for the positions listed below.

manager of a fast food restaurant: _____

_____

_____

server in the same restaurant: _____

_____

_____

_____

coach of a sports team: _____

_____

_____

player on the same team: _____

_____

_____

_____

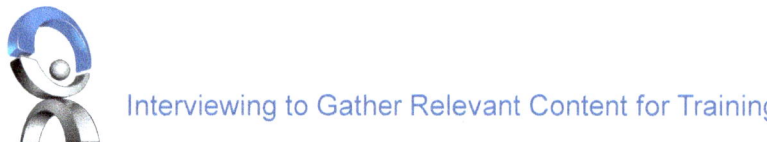

Section 3

Relevant Content Principles

The most important concern for customers is that the content is relevant, useful, and practical so that the resources contribute to their business success. If the content you gather is incomplete or inaccurate, it may be necessary to interview the SME again which can be costly for the customer. Additional interview time also creates scheduling difficulties and the customer may start to doubt your professional capabilities.

To ensure you gather complete and accurate content when interviewing the SME, keep the following principles of relevant content in mind. These principles reinforce the criteria for identifying relevant content described in Section 2—*Use Critical Thinking Strategies to Identify Relevant Content* and address key instructional design considerations.

Key Principles of Relevant Content
• Training is driven by, focuses on, and reinforces corporate objectives/goals.
• All training begins and ends in a job application.
• Training must be targeted to the right audience and tasks.
• Training begins and ends with the worker's frame of reference.

(continued)

Interviewing to Gather Relevant Content for Training

> **Key Principles of Relevant Content**
> - Training must fit the job.
> - Training must complement the organization's structure.
> - Training must reflect the way the organization does business.
> - Training must be corporate, job, and employee focused.
> - Training must be what the customer wants and is willing to pay for.

Training is driven by, focuses on, and reinforces corporate objectives/goals

Driven by—The reason for developing the training in the first place is to contribute to the customer's corporate objectives/goals (i.e., business success).

Focuses on—Corporate objectives/goals identify the types of content that are relevant for the training resources. To be cost-effective and efficient, training is limited to and addresses tasks and support knowledge that directly impact on achieving the corporate objectives (i.e., improves corporate and job performance and reduces the risk of losses).

Reinforces—The training content explains the purpose and importance of doing the tasks, taking action, making decisions, maximizing the use of resources, and minimizing losses. The training process ensures that employees can:
- do the work in accordance with the way the organization does business
- do the work to established standards (expectations)
- make decisions in the organization's best interests

Refer to Section 2.5—*Use a Business Model to Understand the Organization* for additional information about corporate objectives/goals.

All training begins and ends in a job application

Organizations invest in training so that employees can do work more effectively and efficiently and in a way that contributes to business success. At the training program design stage, competencies (tasks and knowledge) important to employee, job, and corporate performance are identified.

Training is then developed and delivered to ensure that the workers can perform the work or do their jobs to the organization's expectations. Worker performance is assessed to confirm that they are competent in doing the work.

Sometimes you may develop training that the customer does not perceive as valuable. It is easy to skew off topic, provide too much detail, or provide *nice to know* content instead of sticking to what the worker needs to know to do his/her job. An important question to ask the SME is, *Does the worker need to know this to do the work safely, effectively, and efficiently?*

The content of knowledge competencies, especially generic competencies, often applies to more than one task. When interviewing the SME to develop knowledge-based training, first identify the tasks that the worker performs where the knowledge is applied. When gathering the content, make sure that the principles, concepts, components, and work or technical processes relate to these tasks.

When developing training for knowledge competencies, provide examples of applying the knowledge to the worker's job. Identifying job applications gives meaning to the knowledge. Identifying how the knowledge affects the worker and the work can provide motivation to learn the content.

Training must be targeted to the right audience and tasks

When determining the focus and scope of the training, either identify the audience or the task first. If you know the audience, their **roles and responsibilities** help you to identify the critical tasks and support knowledge. They also help define the task applications—what the audience can and cannot do and what types of decision the audience can and cannot make.

If you know the task, the roles and responsibilities of different audiences help determine how the task is shared among different types of worker. For example, operators and maintenance personnel may share in the responsibility of performing routine maintenance. However, the expectations of each group for carrying out the maintenance may be different—operators may only do basic maintenance, whereas maintenance workers would perform more complex procedures.

After you have identified the audience and associated task, use the worker's **limits of authority** to further define the task application, performance expectations, and the decisions that are to be made. **Lines and limits of authority, management style**, and **corporate objectives/goals** all provide criteria for worker decision making.

Identifying work conditions, technology, and resources further defines the task and its application.

Training begins and ends with the trainee's frame of reference

After you have identified the audience and the task, identify the audience's qualifications, including experience, skills, and knowledge. For training to be effective and efficient, the training must begin at the trainee's level of ability. You may have an understanding of the trainee's qualifications before interviewing the SME. During the interview, you can further understanding by asking the SME about the trainee's qualifications so that you can determine the trainee's frame of reference:

- hiring and placement qualifications
- work experience
- formal education
- training received through the training program you are developing
- other training previously received from the organization and outside agencies
- cultural and personal attributes (e.g., English as a second language, attitude) that may affect training success

Structured training begins with the trainee's *frame of reference*. At the end of training, the trainee should have a new frame of reference—the experiences, knowledge, skills, and attitudes to perform the tasks in the way that the organization expects.

Training must fit the job

For training to be practical and useful, the training must not only address work and business issues, but also be designed to match the job context. The procedures you develop must begin and end the same way as the work. Tasks or parts of a task that are sequential must be formatted to complement the work sequence and have breaks that logically fit the job. When tasks are sequential, the first action step of the current task logically follows the last action step of the previous task. There are no overlaps or missing steps between sequential tasks or parts of a task. The tasks and training records must be structured to facilitate the assigning of work, training, and practice opportunities.

One valuable strategy for breaking tasks into useful parts that fit the job is to list the tasks or parts of a complex task on a training record. An important question to ask yourself is, *Does the training record help the supervisor assign work, training, and practice opportunities?*

Section 4—*Relevant Content and Instructional Design* identifies pitfalls in designing training to fit the job.

Training must complement the organization's structure

Organizations create structures of job positions so that people and other resources are employed effectively to achieve business goals and complement management styles. When gathering content, you may have to consider coordination issues with other job positions and the impact the work can have on other jobs. When developing work procedures, be careful not to change the worker's roles and responsibilities without your customer's approval.

Sometimes, standards of performance for a specific task may vary between different shifts at one location or between different locations. Different supervisors may have different expectations. For example, one supervisor expects staff to fix a problem when it develops, another supervisor may want to be consulted first; one supervisor may want to be informed about most events on site, another supervisor may only want

to be informed of events that must involve him/her. For training, the standards of performance must apply equally to all shifts and locations. If you find that there are varying expectations in how and how well the work is performed, you may have to ask the customer to resolve the discrepancies.

Different jobs, units, and departments may have conflicting mandates. You must be sensitive to political issues. The customer expects you to avoid escalating issues. You must walk a fine line between escalating issues and clarifying roles and responsibilities and how tasks are to be carried out.

Training must reflect the way the organization does business

Every company has its own way of doing business. If your mandate is to develop training that reflects the way the customer does business, you must pay special attention to these two issues:

- When reviewing information in documents other than those from the customer, do not assume the documents reflect the way your customer does business. If you use the information in the training you develop, you could inadvertently change the way your customer does business. Customers do not want to be told how to do their business.
- Your personal beliefs and values may be different from your customer's. Be aware of your own biases so as not to impose them on your customer. You may not agree with the way the customer does business, but it is most likely not your mandate or responsibility to make changes.

Training must be corporate, job, and employee focused

The resources you develop must have value by contributing to business success—the resources must contribute to improving corporate, job, and employee performance. You must apply criteria for relevant content to each stage of the training program design and development. From conception through to implementation, consideration must be given to ensuring the content is relevant, useful, and practical so that it adds value for the customer. Most training must have a task application and/or contribute to decision making. The corporate objectives provide additional criteria to ensure the training is relevant.

Training must be what the customer wants and is willing to pay for

Because you are a specialist, your customer expects you to make suggestions and provide leadership to identify relevant content. You provide the leadership by asking quality questions relating to corporate, job, and employee performance. From the planning stage through to delivering products, you should regularly confirm with your customer that the content and products are what the customer wants and is willing to pay for.

There may be occasions, however, when you clearly identify content that will contribute to business performance that the customer may not be willing to pay for. You have a responsibility to discuss the benefits of the content with your customer, but keep in mind that your customer has the final say. For example, when developing training resources about equipment, you recommend describing *how the equipment works and how to work the equipment*. There are important relationships between these two concepts that must be addressed so that workers can perform effectively and make decisions in the best interest of the organization. However, your customer may want the resources to address either how the equipment works or how to work the equipment, but not both. Traditions and budgets may be overriding factors that prevent the customer from following your advice. To have satisfied customers (and possibly to keep your job) you need to meet the customer's expectations.

Making recommendations to the customer can also contribute to positive customer relations—you are demonstrating your concern for their wellbeing.

Interviewing to Gather Relevant Content for Training

LEARNING ACTIVITY 9

Relevant content principles

This learning activity helps you understand the importance of applying relevant content principles when interviewing the SME and developing training and reference resources.

Fill out the table below by identifying the potential consequences for the customer if each of the relevant content principles is not applied.

Relevant Content Principle	Potential Consequence if Principle not Applied
Training is driven by, focuses on, and reinforces corporate objectives/goals.	
All training begins and ends in a job application.	
Training must be targeted to the right audience and tasks.	
Training begins and ends with the worker's frame of reference.	
Training must fit the job.	
Training must complement the organization's structure.	
Training must reflect the way the organization does business.	
Training must be corporate, job, and employee focused.	
Training must be what the customer wants and is willing to pay for.	

Section 4
Relevant Content and Instructional Design

The interviewing process described in Part B—*Interviewing to Gather Relevant Content* assumes that:
- the audience has been clearly defined
- the competencies or general training objectives have been identified
- criteria have been used to identify *relevant* competencies or general training objectives
- relevant content criteria have been used to select content for the scope of each competency or general training objective
- the scope of each relevant competency or general training objective has been documented (i.e., content that is important for corporate, job, and employee performance). Generally, the scope for each competency would be a list of eight to twenty key issues a buddy or supervisor would emphasize when coaching the trainee. During the development of the *scope document* attention has been given to ensure continuity between competencies—there are no overlaps or gaps of content between competencies.

- competencies or general training objectives have been arranged in a logical sequence for training
- the structure for the instruction has **not** been developed

These assumptions, however, may not be true. To fill the gap, this section addresses some issues about the relationship of relevant content and instructional design and some pitfalls that you may encounter when gathering content.

4.1 Structure of Training and Reference Resources

Instructional design and content are related. The topics and sequence of the instruction depend on the specific competency or general training objective being addressed.

Boilerplate:
a standard text template that can be used as is or with minor changes for different applications

Sometimes you can use *boilerplates* for specific types of content. A customer may have existing documents that use a boilerplate and you are expected to use their boilerplate when gathering content and developing resources. For training, the boilerplate should incorporate instructional design concepts.

Boilerplates can work well for some reference manuals and for some types of training. For example, a boilerplate can be used to develop training to operate hand-held detection equipment such as gas detectors, thermal imaging equipment, and Geiger counters. The main sections of the instruction are:

1. Introduction
2. Principles of Operation
3. Concepts of Operation
4. Controls and their Function
5. General Operating Procedures
6. Maintenance
7. Troubleshooting

The headings of a boilerplate suggest the *type* of content to be documented. Some boilerplates also suggest the content that could be included in each section with the understanding that not all suggestions would be used for a given application.

PART A Section 4
Relevant Content and Instructional Design

The customer's expectations, audience, and the technology determine the specific types of content that must be addressed.

The advantage of using a boilerplate is that the structure and type of content have already been determined, making content gathering and resource development efficient and ensuring specific types of content will be addressed.

The disadvantage of boilerplates is that, for some competencies, the content may not fit well with the headings of a boilerplate and the content may need to be force-fitted into the structure.

If you do not have a set of boilerplates or the competency does not fit the prescribed boilerplate, you must rely on your experience and skills to structure the training. As part of the interviewing process, you should work with the SME to develop a structure *before* gathering the detailed content. By doing so, you will gather content that is grouped and sequenced, contributing to a more thorough content-gathering process and making the development of training and reference resources more efficient. Just as important, you are also helping to organize the SME's thinking about the content he or she must provide.

4.2 Pitfalls in Designing and Developing Training Programs

In addition to the concerns mentioned in previous sections, the following pitfalls can make it difficult for you to gather relevant content and develop resources.

The Identified Competencies are not Practical for Training

If training program design concepts are not considered when identifying and defining competencies, the resulting competencies may not be useful or practical for training. This problem occurs when designing the training program with minimal consideration for:
- making the training efficient and effective

- ensuring the sequence of training fits the job and is developmental
- assessing competence
- making the administration of training manageable

The result is that some competencies are too large, too small, or do not fit the job. Many of these types of pitfall should be corrected before gathering content. You or others in your organization must work with your customer's decision-makers to modify the training design and get their approval of the changes.

Competency too large

An example of too large a competency is *Manage Projects*. There are several competencies embedded in this larger competency. If a competency is too large, it is very difficult to deliver and track training. The trainee can become discouraged because it may take months to demonstrate competence. Tracking progress is difficult because the tasks and support knowledge for the large competency have likely not been identified in the training record. (Training records often list competencies and assessment methods and not embedded sub-competencies.)

Competency too small

An example of too small a competency is *Check Engine Oil Level*. When there are many small competencies, the training program becomes very large and cumbersome to manage. The training is not efficient in this case because there are other engine checks that could be performed at the same time. In this example, the check engine oil level can be combined with other engine checks.

Isolated Competencies

Generic competencies can be very useful and practical. However, if training for a generic competency is isolated from the tasks where it is applied (e.g., *Couple and Uncouple Hoses or Use Stationary Grinders*), two problems can develop:
- it may be a long time before the learning is applied on the job
- the learning is less effective and practical than if it is built into performing a task

In the case of coupling and uncoupling hoses, safety is an important concern when using air and steam hoses. If the trainee completes generic learning about safety and coupling and uncoupling hoses but does not have an opportunity to apply the learning, the learning has less meaning and may soon be forgotten. It is far more practical and effective to learn to safely couple and uncouple hoses while learning tasks that involve air and steam hoses.

Overlap of content between competencies

If, during the design of the training program, the competencies were not scoped out (i.e., critical content has not been listed for each competency), the content for any given competency is left to interpretation. When developing training, the same content could be addressed in two or more competencies. The result is unnecessary repetition and, more importantly, major difficulties when updating resources. Some generic safety concerns, however, can be repeated between competencies to emphasize their importance.

Instead of repeating specific information to give meaning to the content for a training resource (e.g., training module), consider referencing other training resources.

Sequence of training

It is important to know the sequence of training before interviewing the SME. Often competencies for training are developmental. If you do not know the sequence of training, you may make false assumptions about the trainee's qualifications. You could then gather content that is a repeat of content intended for other competencies or miss content important for learning.

The sequence of training may not have been established by the time you begin gathering content and developing the resources. Some program design strategies do not organize the competencies as a training sequence. Instead, competencies that have something in common are grouped into categories or topics. For example, competencies could be grouped as follows:
- Orientation
- Safety

- Environment
- General Knowledge
- Routine Tasks
- Specific Applications (e.g., leak detection, xyz process, abc mobile equipment)

Using the above organization of competencies as an example, the trainee would not complete all the training for the first category (orientation) and then move to the next category (safety). If this sequence of training were used, it may be more than six months before he or she would do any productive work (routine tasks). Instead, the trainee would complete some training from each category to start work as soon as possible. The competencies need to be reorganized into a series of competencies or new groups for delivering training (e.g., level 1, level 2). Some competencies from each level would be grouped into level 1, other competencies from each level would be grouped into level 2, and so on.

When interviewing, if the SME is not familiar with the training program design, you should discuss the program and identify the competencies related to the one for which you will be gathering content. Other competencies may be prerequisites or vice versa. The training sequence affects the type of content gathered for each competency.

In some cases, there may be basic and advanced training for a task. The advanced level usually requires more knowledge, and the application of the task may be more challenging. You need to understand the difference between basic and advanced training so that the content you gather is appropriate for the intended level.

Repetition of content of competencies that are similar

Sometimes technology at several different sites is similar but the application of technology is somewhat different for each site, for example, gas wellsites, where each gas well may behave differently. The size of equipment and its configuration will therefore vary from wellsite to wellsite. However, having learned how to monitor and operate equipment at a complex wellsite, the trainee can learn the

PART A Section 4
Relevant Content and Instructional Design

differences for other wellsites. You can take either of the following instructional design approaches:

1. Provide generic training about how each piece of equipment operates. The trainee then learns about the specific variables and the operation of equipment at each site.

2. Provide training for a complex site, including how the equipment operates, the variables, and how to operate the equipment. The trainee then goes to other, less complex sites and learns the operating differences. There is no need to explain how the equipment operates for every site. The training focuses on the variables and how to operate the equipment specific to each site.

Omission of critical content

During content gathering, critical content may be identified that should have been included in the training that has already been developed. Backtracking to fill the gaps in existing training adds cost to program development. A scope document helps reduce the likelihood of omitting critical content. Discussing the type of content for different competencies with the SME can also help in identifying omissions.

The mix of content between competencies does not fit well with the job

Even when the scope of each competency has been worked out in detail, this problem can occasionally arise when you gather the detailed content. The content for the competencies may have to be reorganized to make the training practical and fit the work. For example, a basic and an advanced competency have been identified for training on gas detection systems:

- *Describe* Fixed Gas Detection Systems and Alarms
- *Monitor* Fixed Gas Detection Systems

While gathering content, it is determined that, when a person first starts work, the critical issue is to be able to respond to gas detector alarms. Training to be able to describe the gas detection components and monitor the systems is important but this training is provided later. The decision to make the competencies match better with the work requires the

content and titles of the competencies to be changed:
- *Respond* to Fixed Gas Detector Alarms
- *Describe* and *Monitor* Fixed Gas Detection Systems

 Be sure to inform the person responsible for building the training records about changes to the competency titles and methods of assessment.

Support knowledge for tasks and decision making is fragmented

For entry level training that puts a strong emphasis on performing tasks (i.e., work processes), the knowledge to prepare trainees to do the tasks can be included with each task. For each task, there may be two to four pages explaining:
- conditions requiring the task to be performed
- desired results
- major steps to the task
- safety concerns
- how to perform specific steps efficiently
- how to respond to abnormal circumstances

For technical processes, operating the technology may involve several tasks. If some of the knowledge is provided with each task, the continuity and overall picture of how the technology operates is fragmented. Often a knowledge module about how the technology operates and how to operate the technology is desirable to maintain the continuity of information.

Procedures for the tasks would be developed separately from the knowledge-based module.

The SME wants to add content

Sometimes an SME may be adamant about adding content that appears to be *nice to know*. The concern is how much value the additional content will add to the worker's performance. The issue can become significant if there will be a considerable cost to develop the suggested content or if the scope of a competency has already been developed. For example, you are interviewing an SME on how to monitor and maintain thermal electric generators. The SME has been performing the work satisfactorily but does not understand how the electricity is generated and thinks knowing might be of value to a trainee. To develop the content, you would have to do a literature search. Discuss with the SME the value of adding the content versus the cost to develop it. If the scope for the competency already exists, then those who developed it should be consulted. An alternative to satisfy the SME's interest may be to find the information for the SME but not include the information in the training resources.

You think you can develop the training with minimal input from the SME

You may have previously developed similar training to what is needed for your current project. Familiarity with the material may lead you to believe that you can develop the training resources with minimal input from the SME. In some cases, especially for **generic** training, you may be correct; if so, you can save time.

When your existing knowledge of similar content can reduce the time to gather content, make sure to get the SME's agreement on training content and outcomes.

Missing information

For **site-specific** training on equipment and processes, you should take the time to gather detailed content from the SME. If you do **not** gather the relevant details:
- you may not have all the information needed and will have to do excessive research or re-interview the SME to fill the gaps in the content
- you may need to make major changes to the structure of the document because you started writing before you had all the necessary information

In either case, you could spend a lot more time trying to fill gaps and restructuring content than if you had gathered detailed content from the SME in the first place.

If you do not gather the site-specific details, you may find that

Interviewing to Gather Relevant Content for Training

you do not know enough to write the module; for example:
- The equipment's make and model is different from the ones for which you developed training in the past.
- The equipment configuration (e.g., for a technical process) is different from the ones you previously worked on, and it operates (and is operated) differently.
- The process system and the operating variables and settings are unique to the site.
- The response of equipment or system to changing conditions is unique to the site.
- The indicators for abnormal operation and the worker's expected response are unique to the site.
- Company policies directing worker responses are unique to the organization and site.

Be very careful when trying to save time by using content from a training program developed for a different organization. Roles and responsibilities, policies, and supervisor expectations may be different. The training you develop using content from another program could change the way the organization does business—organizations do not want to be told how to do business by outsiders.

Unique operating strategies

Experienced workers at different sites may use different operating and decision-making strategies. Some operating strategies are complex, requiring the worker to assess many variables in one or more systems to effectively respond to changes. The worker may have to decide:
- the operational change(s) to make, to what degree, and how rapidly to make the change(s)
- monitoring requirements throughout the system(s) to:
  - confirm that the operational change has the desired effect
  - observe that the change has limited or acceptable tradeoffs between variables (e.g., product flow rates to two different streams)
  - determine the additional operational changes required when the results are excessive or insufficient

PART A Section 4
Relevant Content and Instructional Design

Ambiguous terms

When interviewing SMEs about site-specific operating strategies, the SME may use terms such as: *as required*, *as needed*, or *appropriate* to describe strategies involving decision making. When ambiguous terms are used, you need to establish whether the trainee has the prerequisite training to make the decision. Ask the SME what is involved in the decision-making process so you can determine how to design/develop the training. To explain the decision-making process, you might consider presenting:

- scenarios that could or have actually taken place at that site
- normal operation scenarios to help the trainee determine when adjustments are not required

The SME may give you memos or operating practice documents that he or she feels describes the operating and decision-making strategies. Work through the memos or practices with the SME to ensure you capture the relevant content because these types of document may:

- be based on unstated assumptions
- be outdated
- have limited application because they no longer apply as universally as before

Unsuitable training structure

One of the difficulties encountered when developing training for complex responses to abnormal operation is determining a suitable structure for training that is developmental. If you only take minimal notes, you might develop a structure for the training that does not work for detailed instruction.

By tentatively deciding on how the training will be designed and delivered, you will be able to effectively develop a structure for gathering the content and gathering quality content. Take the time with the SME to gather the content in the structure in which it will be presented to the trainee.

Program Design and Development Challenges

You may have to consult with the person responsible for the training you are developing (e.g., site supervisor) to determine the best solution for challenges like the following.

As-builts—should content be developed for *the way it is* or *the way it will be?*

While gathering content, the SME may point out that the facility is being upgraded. Do you develop training for the existing facility or for the upgraded facility? There are two main issues:
- the additional investment to update the training resources for the existing facility and then again for the upgraded facility.
- the length of time before the upgrades to the facility have been completed

Consider discussing the issues with the site supervisor or others responsible for training.

The customer may not be in compliance with regulation

When gathering content, you may discover that the SME evades some issues about how the work is performed. For example:
- Regulations require that two people must carry out specific tasks but only one person is assigned to night shift when the task may have to be performed.
- Regulations require that at least two people must be on shift at all times to operate the emergency vehicle, but only one person is scheduled for some shifts.

The organization would not want you to document training content that does not comply with regulation. On the other hand, you cannot complete the training resources without resolving the issue. You will have to take your concerns to the organization's management and let them determine how to interpret the regulations and decide how you should word the content.

Assumption that the training profile of competencies is a job description

Most training programs are a sub-set of all competencies relating to the roles and responsibilities for a particular

PART A   Section 4
Relevant Content and Instructional Design

position. However, sometimes the training profile is structured according to the technology, not job positions. Perhaps the organization wants people to be trained in tasks that are not part of their normal jobs so there is more flexibility in placing staff. In some cases, competencies may also prepare a person for advancement.

Nevertheless, some SMEs may think that the written training profile of competencies defines the roles and responsibilities for a specific job position. Stating that the profile is a job description may create a discrepancy with established job descriptions. Your best strategy is to point out that the training profile covers many—but not all—of the roles and responsibilities for the position. You may also point out that, when a person is being assessed for job performance, in addition to satisfactorily completing the training, other performance issues not listed on the profile may also be considered. For example, performance appraisals may also consider behaviors such as getting to work on time, getting along with others, being accountable, and taking personal initiative.

SME wants to use training standards to fire someone

As a training consultant or technical writer, you have a responsibility for ensuring customer satisfaction. Part of this responsibility is to ensure there is value in the resources you are developing by doing quality work and by promoting the benefits of the resources for the users. You need to ensure that the purpose of the training is to be supportive in improving performance and not a tool to reprimand anyone. Consider presenting the following argument for not using training standards to fire someone.

For training to have the most value, it must be perceived as beneficial and supportive in improving performance. Using the training standards as a tool to fire someone is detrimental to the goals of training. If training standards were to be used to reprimand workers, workers could develop a negative attitude towards participating in the training program.

There can be many reasons for poor performance, including problems outside of work or health issues. Due process should be used to determine the cause. If lack of competence is the issue, then training can be provided. If the person proves to have major difficulties in learning to do the work safely and effectively, then decisions can be made as to his/her future employment. One option is to place the worker in a different job that better matches his or her abilities.

SME expresses work-related dissatisfaction

Your SME may complain about the organization, the work, other people, or other departments. Acknowledge what he or she says but do not express your own opinion or agree/disagree. Do not get caught up in corporate politics. One way to acknowledge the person is to paraphrase what was said. Openers to paraphrasing include:

You're saying...

You're telling me..

Documentation is for both training and reference

Training and reference documents are structured quite differently and typically include different types of information. A problem arises when the client wants the materials to serve *both* purposes.

For training, technical information is limited to and focuses on supporting task performance and decision making. The presentation of training content also uses instructional design techniques such as advanced organizers (e.g., an overview), headings, and transitions to facilitate comprehension and long-term retention of the information.

Reference manuals usually provide detailed technical information and specifications. Indexes may be included to help find specific information. Because the goals and content of reference manuals are different from training manuals, the structure of the reference manuals is also different.

Some customers may want the documentation to be useful for training and for reference. To a limited degree, the presentation of content can be adjusted to accommodate both training and reference goals. Use a structure that is primarily for training. For transition of topics, only use headings; do not use transition paragraphs. Bulleted and numbered lists reduce the amount of text, provide detailed information, and help readers mentally organize the material. Appendices can be used for referencing specifications. An expanded table of contents and/or an index helps the user locate information.

Variable specifications change

One of the difficulties in specifying variables and their actual settings in training and reference documents is that some settings may change, depending on the season or site event. Updating settings in the training resources can be difficult, especially when they are stated in several different places. To prevent the need to continually update the documents:

- state that the settings can change and that the training/reference information provides approximations or ranges to facilitate understanding only
- identify where information on the current settings can be found (e.g., appendix which only lists the settings once or on a control room computer)

Developing training for the least qualified trainee

Usually, training is developed for the least qualified person entering the job position. Defining the entry qualifications of trainees could become troublesome when gathering the detailed content, especially for maintenance training programs. Four key factors must be considered in determining what the trainee already knows and can do:

- The organization's job placement criteria. For the job position, does the organization select journeymen or apprentices?
- The experience of journeymen. The journeyman's work experience may not match the requirements for the job. For example, a millwright who previously worked in sawmills is now going to work in a petrochemical facility; an electrician has experience in wiring residential homes and is now going to do industrial work.
- Some journeymen continue to learn year after year to keep up with changes in technology; other journeymen do not.
- Sometimes organizations move workers from a related position with the assumption that much of their learning is

transferable. Their knowledge and experience may not be as transferable as originally thought.

Often, the main purpose of training is to improve the competence of existing workers. When gathering detailed content for training, you need to question the assumptions about the qualifications of existing workers. Keep in mind that the training is targeted to a group, not to any specific worker. Knowing the previous job positions of workers can also help you decide whether or not to include specific details in the training materials.

For new hires, unless there is a specific change in hiring and placement criteria and economics, existing worker qualifications are representative of future worker qualifications for placement.

SME is *not* qualified to provide the content

The ease of gathering content and the quality of gathered content depends upon you and your SME's abilities. You can provide a great deal of direction and leadership if you clearly understand:
- the training outcomes that are desired, and
- the criteria for selecting training content that contributes to the training outcomes

If the SME is highly qualified to provide the content, the content-gathering process should go smoothly. The SME will not only be able to provide specific information, but will also be able to provide some direction as to the specific issues that should or should not be addressed in the training resources. However, having an ideal SME doesn't always happen.

Sometimes supervisors do not want to release their most experienced worker to be an SME. Instead, they provide you with an SME who does not have adequate experience or knowledge to provide quality content. Sometimes, an experienced and knowledgeable worker may struggle to explain the content.

Often the SME has one or more of the following weaknesses:
- has no clear understanding of the acceptable standards for performing the tasks

- has no clear understanding of the key issues impacting the company, the job, and workers (i.e., what's important and what's not important)
- is operating at a high level of understanding and has developed general strategies for doing the work and solving work-related problems. The SME has generalized his or her understanding and has forgotten the specific technology and learning difficulties he or she went through to reach the generalized level of understanding.
- may be very visual and have difficulties putting ideas into words
- may be a simultaneous thinker. The SME can recall all kinds of ideas at one time and has difficulty sorting and grouping the information and identifying relevant information.
- can be impatient or preoccupied. The SME may have forgotten about any difficulties and stresses he or she went through to be good at the job, was an exceptionally fast learner, or may have exceptionally high expectations as to the abilities of untrained workers. This type of SME would most likely say something like: *If the trainee doesn't know that, he shouldn't be working here.*

Even if the SME is weak in providing relevant and accurate content, the most effective way for you to compensate is to provide leadership to identify and organize relevant content and ask pertinent questions.

When it becomes apparent that your SME is struggling to provide quality content, consider talking to the supervisor to have the SME replaced with a more qualified person. Efforts should be made to make the change in a way that salvages the replaced SME's esteem and to maintain the target audience's acceptance of the training program as being useful and beneficial.

Poor content-gathering environment

A supervisor may not be willing to release an SME full time to be dedicated to working with you. Your SME may receive constant interruptions such as phone calls from site personnel or leave to deal with job issues. The content-gathering process

Interviewing to Gather Relevant Content for Training

can become very inefficient because of lost time. Every time the SME is interrupted, he or she has to rethink the content when the interview resumes. The quality of the content you gather can also be compromised.

The investment or cost to develop training can increase considerably and a program budget can be a very sensitive issue. You need to explain to the supervisor the problems created when the SME is not given dedicated time to work for you. Consider putting your discussion with the supervisor in writing (e.g., sending an e-mail). If budgets become a concern, you have a paper trail to back up your difficulties in gathering content.

The place for conducting the interview can also make it difficult to concentrate on gathering content. For example, coffee rooms have lots of distractions. Alternatives may be to use a quieter area on site or an office that someone has temporarily vacated, setting up at a hotel, or having the SME travel to your office.

Gathering Content as Draft Procedures

You may have to gather content for procedures. If planned well, you can gather the content for the procedures in a way that is almost a finished draft. Only some refinement to the wording and formatting may be required to finalize the draft. The information that follows can help you be more effective in gathering the content for procedures.

Procedures must provide clear direction so that workers learn to do the tasks safely, effectively, and efficiently. Some supervisors believe it is better to have no procedure for a task than to have a poorly written one. Their arguments are:
- when a worker believes the procedure has been thoroughly tested and is correct, the tendency is to let his or her guard down in thinking through the task and not considering what can go wrong
- a poorly written procedure has the potential of causing harm to PEMEO

You must use specific criteria to ensure that the procedures are correct and useful and minimize ambiguity. You must

know the purpose and target audience so that you write the procedures at the required level of detail, For example, the purpose may be:
- to establish a standard for experienced workers
- to train workers new to the position
- for reference

Procedures for experienced workers require fewer details than procedures used for training. When providing detailed action steps for training, be careful not to be so detailed that no one will want to use them. Keep in mind that the trainer or buddy will be demonstrating how to carry out each step. Sometimes it is more effective and efficient to *demonstrate* the actions than to give a detailed explanation of the procedure.

Initially, trainees require detailed action steps while learning the procedure. However, as they become better at performing the task, they may prefer to have a less detailed procedure. One way to address both levels is to use major steps with five to seven detailed action steps per major step. (However, more than seven steps may be required at times to maintain continuity.) For example, the major steps for starting a pipeline pump station may be:

1. Carry out pre-start checks.
2. Start booster pumps.
3. Start main pumps.
4. Increase throughput.
5. Monitor station operation.

For each major step, list the detailed action steps required to complete the major step.

As the trainees become more experienced, they only need to read the major steps and perform the related steps. If they are uncertain about how to carry out a major step, they can refer to the detailed action steps.

This procedure format is also useful for experienced workers who have not done the task for a long period of

Interviewing to Gather Relevant Content for Training

time (e.g., providing vacation relief). They can follow the major steps and refer to the detailed action steps if they have forgotten how to carry out a major step.

NOTE A written procedure is always used for some critical tasks. Each step of the procedure is checked off as the steps are completed. For example, pilots use a written checklist when performing pre-flight checks.

Detailed procedures are also useful when the coaching process is not very effective. A coach may use the written procedure to tell and show the trainee and then the trainee is expected to use the written procedure to carry out the task without supervision.

Sometimes SMEs do not want detailed procedures. Explain the importance of providing step-by-step procedures and the pitfalls of making assumptions about the trainee's ability. Get agreement on the number of major steps; you may have to compromise on the number of detailed steps.

To develop a rough draft of the procedure, use the template or format that will be used for the final procedures.

1. Fill in the header information, especially the title of the task, the discipline (or audience), and the date.

2. Before recording the procedure:
   - ask the SME to explain the purpose and importance of the task and give a general description about how the task is performed. This information gives you an overview of the task.
   - ask the SME to tell you the critical issues involved with performing the task to achieve the desired results and to prevent potential losses. You need this information to identify the need for cautions and warnings.

3. Collaboratively, identify and record the major steps of the task. The major steps help the SME organize his or her thoughts about how the task is performed.

4. Record the specific action steps for each major step.

 For some tasks, a critical task analysis may be required to identify potential hazards and controls to reduce the probability of an incident occurring and/or the severity of the consequences.

It is very important to have new procedures validated. You may also need specialists, such as safety advisors, to review the procedures.

Usefulness of checklists for monitoring equipment

Checklists are often used when checking equipment operation. Items on these checklists must be grouped so that the user does not have to do unnecessary walking to do the checks. This problem can arise when developing equipment checklists for technical processes and power generation facilities. Process equipment may not always be located in one area. The process flow lines may go from one piece of equipment to another and then loop back to the area where the first piece of equipment is located. If the checklist is developed by following the process, the user may have to walk back and forth or between floors several times. If workers and trainees have to do unnecessary walking, they may conclude that the checklist is not very practical. A more efficient way to check equipment is to develop the checklist for an area, even if the equipment is not related to a single process.

Process sequence does not match roles and responsibilities

Job positions often match the technology. For example, in a gas plant there may be several operator positions. Each position aligns with one process system (e.g., inlet separation and compression, dehydration, fractionation). Because process flowlines may loop back and forth, some equipment from one process may be located close to another process. As an example, in the compression area, there may be a vessel that belongs to another process. The compressor operator may have the responsibility of monitoring that vessel. When developing training, you could provide the area operator with the knowledge and procedures to operate and monitor the compressors but only the procedures to monitor the vessel. The knowledge about how the vessel works can be addressed when developing training for the other process.

Interviewing to Gather Relevant Content for Training

LEARNING ACTIVITY 10

Relevant content and instructional design

This learning activity helps you to be more effective at interviewing the SME to develop training that is relevant, useful, and practical.

The planning and interviewing process has many pitfalls. Being aware of the pitfalls and possible solutions can help you to be better prepared to develop relevant, useful, and practical training.

1. You will likely not be confronted with all of the pitfalls identified in this book. From the following list, check the pitfalls you would most likely encounter.

    - ☐ supervisors disagree about how and how well to perform the work
    - ☐ the boiler plate format does not work well with the type of content or desired outcomes of training
    - ☐ competency too large
    - ☐ competency too small
    - ☐ isolated competencies
    - ☐ overlap of content between competencies
    - ☐ sequence of training not identified
    - ☐ repetition of content of competencies that are similar
    - ☐ omission of content
    - ☐ the mix of content within the competency or between competencies does not fit well with the job
    - ☐ the support knowledge for tasks and decision making is fragmented
    - ☐ the SME wants to add content
    - ☐ you think you can develop the training with minimal input from the SME
    - ☐ develop content for the way it is or the way it will be
    - ☐ the customer may not operate in compliance with legislation

☐ SME assumes the training profile of competencies is a job description

☐ SME wants to use training standards to fire someone

☐ SME complains about work-related issues

☐ documentation is for training and reference

☐ developing training for the least qualified trainee

☐ SME is not qualified to provide the content

☐ using external SMEs

☐ poor content-gathering environment

☐ level of detail of procedures

☐ usefulness of checklists for monitoring equipment

☐ process sequence does not match roles and responsibilities

2. From the previous list of pitfalls, select three you are most likely to encounter and explain how you might deal with the problem.

Pitfall 1: _____

Possible solution: _____

_____

_____

_____

Pitfall 2: _____

Possible solution: _____

_____

_____

_____

Interviewing to Gather Relevant Content for Training

Pitfall 3: _____

Possible solution: _____

_____

_____

_____

PART B

Interviewing to Gather Relevant Content

Using effective consulting and instructional design and development processes, you can develop quality training for a variety of disciplines and technologies. To do so, you must provide leadership when working with SMEs to identify content important for training—content that contributes to corporate, job, and employee performance. You do not need to know much about the discipline or technology to be successful. However, you do need to be able to identify important performance issues. By applying a variety of critical thinking strategies described in Part A, you can identify relevant, useful, and practical content for training.

There are three basic ways to identify relevant content:
- conduct a literature search
- provide the content yourself, based on your experience
- interview your customer's experienced staff, contractors, manufacturers, and vendors (SMEs). This interviewing process is called *gathering content*.

The way you identify relevant content should not influence your product; any of these three methods should produce similar results. However, interviewing your customer's staff will provide more site-specific content that other sources cannot provide.

Part B provides detailed directions and helpful hints for conducting interviews to gather relevant content. The fundamental premises of Part B are:
- You need to identify relevant content, group and sequence the content, and develop training resources and assessment instruments for knowledge and tasks.
- The customer expects you to provide leadership to identify relevant, useful, and practical content.
- You do not need significant knowledge of the customer's technology and tasks to provide leadership in identifying relevant content and developing effective training resources.
- You can apply critical thinking strategies to identify relevant content.
- The interviewing process involves asking quality questions to identify relevant content.

Benefits of Interviewing

Interviewing the customer's SMEs is the best way to identify relevant content. Interviewing requires a lot of customer involvement, but has many benefits:
- Because the people who do the work know their company and their jobs the best, the content you gather during an interview closely reflects the customer's realities. For example:
    - workplace
    - customer specific equipment
    - roles and responsibilities
    - ways of working
    - communication requirements
    - policies
    - management style
    - decision-making protocols
    - business strategies

PART B
Interviewing to Gather Relevant Content

You can document site-specific applications and examples and select language and terms that are appropriate for the customer.
- Through discussion with the customer's staff, you can get a good understanding of the trainee's experiences, knowledge, and abilities. This understanding helps you determine the types of information that should be addressed, the amount of detail required, and the required reading level.
- Because the customer's staff are directly involved in the development of the training program, getting their input helps to develop their ownership of the product. As a result, they are more likely to accept the program as being beneficial for both themselves and their company (i.e., developing buy-in to the program).

Refer to Attachment 1—*Purpose and Benefits of Interviewing the Customer's Experienced Staff* for a complete list of the purposes and benefits of interviewing the customer's workers and supervisors to identify relevant training content.

Drawbacks of Interviewing

Interviewing can also have drawbacks:
- Interviews may take days or weeks. Scheduling one or more continuous blocks of time with the SME can be difficult. Customers rely on their experienced staff to meet specialized work requirements and are often unwilling to relieve them of work assignments for as long as it takes to provide content.
- If the SME is not effective in providing information, the interview can take longer than anticipated and the quality of content gathered may not be satisfactory. Some SMEs may be simultaneous thinkers, very visual, or weak at grouping and sequencing information. Over time, they may create generalities of complex information to make their jobs easier. They may have also forgotten the detail and what it was like to be a trainee. Some SMEs are very fast learners and cannot appreciate the difficulties other learners may have. These SMEs usually have difficulties in

identifying content important for training, organizing their thoughts, and communicating effectively.
- Interviews may not be efficient or effective for identifying specific types of content (e.g., principles of operation):
  - The available literature may provide an accurate description of principles and equipment.
  - The interviewing process may interfere with your ability to concentrate on understanding the principles and on determining the best way to present the information in the training material. Providing effective instruction on principles can be difficult, and you may need to pay special attention to the development of ideas and presentation of instruction (e.g., by using analogies and conceptual drawings).

Importance of Effective Interviewing

The interview is a cooperative process in which you and the SME use your individual expertise to identify the content for the training material. You have the performance, training, educational, and writing expertise to provide direction and leadership to ensure that all the relevant content is identified. The SME knows the company and job and provides the specific information required for the training resources.

To meet your customer's expectations, it is essential to gather content that is accurate, complete, and relevant to the tasks that the workers perform and the decisions they make. Gathering quality content makes development of quality training resources an efficient process that requires little rework or additional research.

However, if you gather inaccurate, incomplete, or irrelevant content, your peers may not be able to help you, the cost to develop the resources increases dramatically, your customer may be dissatisfied with your product, and your credibility may be questioned.

As you complete each section of Part B about interviewing, you may want to refer to the Attachments at the end of the book as a summary for that section. You can also use many of the attachments as job aids while conducting interviews.

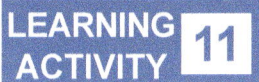

Benefits and drawbacks of interviewing SMEs

When you understand the purpose and importance of the interviewing process to gather relevant content, you will be more effective at interviewing SMEs.

The following questions apply to normal conditions unless otherwise stated. From the given choices, select the best answer to each question. Although other choices may apply under different conditions, do not consider these choices as being the best answers.

1. Interviewing the customer's experienced workers to gather content helps you to _____.
    a. document practical applications of concepts
    b. select language appropriate for the customer
    c. determine the type of information that should be addressed in the training resources
    d. determine the amount of detail and reading level required for the training resources
    e. all of the above

2. The interviewing process is beneficial to customers because it promotes worker involvement in and acceptance of the training program.
    a. true
    b. false

3. Interviewing the customer's experienced staff (SMEs) can be **ineffective** because_____.
    a. scheduling large blocks of time with SMEs can be difficult
    b. the SME may not be effective in providing content
    c. the content can be more easily obtained from a book or other literature
    d. all of the above

4. The development of training resources for industry requires in-depth knowledge of the subject matter and the job.

   a. true
   b. false

5. Interviewing to gather content is a cooperative process in which the consultant or technical writer and the SME each use their respective expertise to identify relevant content.

   a. true
   b. false

6. The purpose of interviewing SMEs is to identify and structure relevant content so that the _____.

   a. training will improve peoples' performances
   b. workforce's structure and roles can be redesigned
   c. information will help in writing training and reference resources
   d. a and b
   e. a and c

Answer Key

1. e
2. a
3. d
4. b
5. a
6. e

Section 5

Planning Interviewing Sessions

Careful planning is critical for conducting successful interviews. You may be part of a team developing training and your team leader may be responsible for some of the planning. This section assumes that you will do all the planning. Other assumptions are listed at the beginning of Section 4—*Relevant Content and Instructional Design*.

The initial planning involves a meeting between you and the customer to establish a work plan. The planning includes:
- confirming criteria and methods for identifying relevant training content. Most likely, the criteria will contribute to performing tasks and making decisions. If relevant content criteria were used to develop the program outline, the list of corporate objectives has most likely been developed. If you must develop the list of corporate objectives, make sure to use the customer's terms. Although many organizations have similar corporate objectives, the priorities and exact language of the corporate objectives varies among customers. The list of corporate objectives/goals must be used during the interview.
- identifying potential interviewers (you), SMEs and validators
- selecting an effective SME

- establishing roles and responsibilities of you and your customer's staff
- discussing the type of on-site work space needed to conduct the interviews
- discussing the interviewing, training resource development, and validation processes
- establishing work objectives and timelines
- establishing reporting procedures
- establishing a start date
- identifying and booking accommodation (e.g., motel) and making travel arrangements. To ensure availability, accommodation and travel arrangements should be booked several weeks before the site visit.
- getting directions to the site
- preparing the SME for the interview sessions

5.1 Selecting the SME

You likely do not have authority or personal knowledge to select your SMEs. However, you can make strong recommendations as to the SME's desirable qualifications. Emphasize the benefits/consequences of effective and ineffective SMEs.

Qualifications of an effective SME include:
- comprehensive on-the-job experience related to the job position
- interest in training other employees
- ability to communicate effectively
- ability to organize ideas and information
- availability for the duration of the interview process and able to provide his/her complete and undivided attention during the interview
- respected by employees within the organization, including supervisors, peers, and subordinates. If well respected, the SME will be able to encourage other employees to accept the training program as being useful and beneficial, and will help make the training content credible.

Having identified SMEs, confirm their qualifications with the customer.

PART B Section 5
Planning Interviewing Sessions

5.2 Preparing the SME for the Interview

Once the SME has been selected and the scope of work specified, contact the SME to:
- establish a meeting time
- discuss the work assignment
- instruct the SME to bring useful resources to the interview (e.g., operations manuals, vendor manuals, process drawings, written procedures, operating and maintenance monitoring records)
- send the scope document or outlines to the SME
- if completed training resources (e.g., modules) are already developed for the customer and are similar to the resources being developed, you may wish to provide samples to the SME. Before the interview, the SME can review the material to understand what a finished product looks like and get a sense of the type of content required for training.

5.3 Preparing for the Interview

Preparing for the interview involves three activities:
- determining training outcomes and type of content
- gathering computer equipment and documentation
- selecting work and safety clothing

Determining training outcomes and type of content

You initially need to know only a little about the job or the specific content for a training resource provided you understand the application outcomes of the training (tasks and decisions) and can ask the right types of question (apply relevant content criteria addressed in Part A). Before interviewing your SME, you should have a basic understanding of:
- the customer's mission and strategic business objectives
- list of corporate objectives. Corporate objectives are essential in identifying content that is relevant and content that should **not** be included in the documentation.
- the customer's training goals and training program scope
- the specific type of technology used by the customer
- basic concepts relating to the customer's technology or processes

113

Interviewing to Gather Relevant Content for Training

- the training audience
- tasks performed by the target audience
- qualifications of the target audience including
  - formal education
  - experience at the job
  - prerequisite training
- scope of the work
- relationship between the training that you will develop and the rest of the customer's training program

Gathering computer equipment and documentation

Sometimes an SME will come to your office but usually you will meet the SME at the worksite. Take the following resources to the interview site:

- laptop computer, data backup memory and, as an option, a printer
- stationery
- support documents
- list of criteria for relevant content
- intrinsically safe camera (if working in an area where flammable gas or dust is present)

Refer to Attachment 2—*Project and Interview Preparation Checklists* which lists the resources to take to the interview.

You must be able to troubleshoot and correct minor computer problems should they arise. If you need to print a document on site, check beforehand to ensure a printer will be available.

There is always the possibility that the SME may not be able to attend the meeting at the scheduled time or may have to leave the meeting to deal with work issues. Take along other project work that you can do while you wait.

Selecting work and safety clothing

For the first meeting, determining the appropriate dress code can be difficult as there are five different sets of dress code expectations that must be considered:

- representing your organization professionally
- meeting the expectations of the customer's management as to the image that you should portray

PART B Section 5
Planning Interviewing Sessions

- matching the SME's dress code to develop rapport
- preventing good clothes from being soiled or damaged
- complying with worksite safety clothing requirements and ensuring personal safety

Some locations may expect formal business attire, while at other sites, jeans and work boots are more appropriate. If there is any uncertainty as to the dress code, you may want to ask the customer before heading to the site.

Whether you need to tour the site or not, most industrial sites require safety footwear and other personal safety equipment such as:
- eye protection
- hearing protection
- fire resistant coveralls
- hard hat

Check with the customer to determine the safety equipment they can provide and the safety equipment you need to bring with you.

Site employees make a special effort to ensure that visitors are kept out of harm's way. Some customers will prefer you to use their visitor hard hats so that employees can easily identify you as a visitor.

Contractual agreements and insurance coverage may restrict your activities. Many customers require visitors to tour their sites under the supervision of a site employee. Insurance restrictions may include *you* **not** being allowed to take pictures.

Planning the interviewing sessions

Careful planning for the interview sessions contributes to successful interviews to gather relevant, useful, and practical content.

The following questions apply to normal conditions unless otherwise stated. From the given choices, select the best answer to each question. Although other choices may apply under different conditions, do not consider these choices as being the best answers.

1. The qualification(s) for an effective SME is/are: _____.

    a. comprehensive on-the-job experience
    b. interest in training other employees
    c. ability to communicate effectively
    d. respect from supervisors, peers, and subordinates
    e. all of the above
    f. a and b only

2. Before interviewing an SME, you must understand the customer's _____.

    a. mission and strategic business objectives
    b. training goals and training program scope
    c. technology
    d. employees who will be receiving training, including their education, job experiences, and job tasks
    e. all of the above

3. If an SME has to leave an interview to deal with critical work problems, you should _____.

    a. ask the site supervisor to provide another SME
    b. go with the SME if at all possible
    c. have other project work on hand
    d. ask other customer staff for a tour of the site

4. What personal safety equipment should be considered for a site tour?

    a. safety footwear
    b. eye and hearing protection
    c. coveralls and a hard hat
    d. all of the above
    e. a and c only

Answer Key
1. e
2. e
3. c
4. d

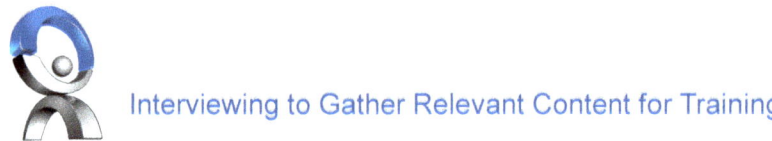
Interviewing to Gather Relevant Content for Training

Section 6

Conducting the Interview

The interviewing process used to gather training content is somewhat similar to the interviewing process used to gather information for a newspaper or news broadcast. The interviewer asks lots of questions. The SME provides lots of answers. However, there are also differences between the two interviewing processes. The interviewing process to gather training content is a cooperative effort between you and the SME.

Throughout the interview, keep your responsibilities and the objectives of the interview in mind:
- provide leadership to identify relevant, useful, and practical content
- gather relevant content
- structure the content
- identify assessment items, especially for knowledge
- portray the training program as valuable and useful for the target audience

The interviewing process to gather training content consists of five major steps (shown in the following illustration).

 Interviewing to Gather Relevant Content for Training

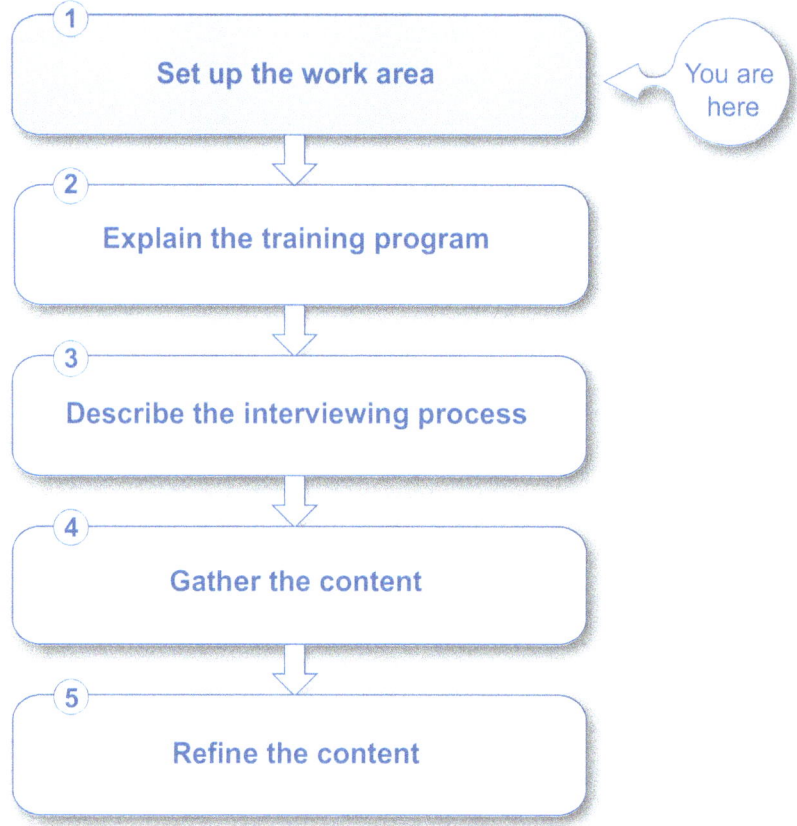

Attachment 3—*Interviewing Checklist* summarizes the interviewing steps explained in this book.

When working with the SME, you may want to make some adjustments to the interviewing process to gather content depending on:
- the willingness of the SME to gather information or prepare a rough draft for some of the content
- your ability to provide some generic training content (i.e., because of your expertise or by using similar training documents)

Major Step 1—Set up the Work Area

On the first day of the interview, arrive on site a bit early. There may be some delays in getting through security and finding the correct meeting place. Security at sites varies, from no security whatsoever, to signing in and out, to having to wear a security tag and be escorted to the specific location. Make sure you have the names and phone numbers of the SME and supervisor when passing through security. Some sites require you to complete a one-half to four-hour safety course before being allowed on site.

Generally, the first person you meet will be a supervisor or team leader. He or she will introduce the SME and identify the work area. It's best if the interview takes place near the SME's work area because:
- the SME will be more at ease in familiar surroundings
- related documents are often close to the work area
- you and the SME can easily go to the work area to look at the technology or observe a task being performed

The location must have adequate heat, light, and ventilation. Whenever possible, the interview should not take place in the office of the SME's supervisor. This location could lead the SME to associate you with "management," inhibiting the SME from being candid and straightforward.

Sometimes the customer has difficulty providing a suitable work area. It may be necessary to set up in a coffee room or in someone's office that has been vacated for the day. It is not uncommon to have to move to different locations during the site visit. If setting up in someone's office, try to clear a work area in a way that causes minimal disturbance. For the first meeting, arrange the work area so that the SME **cannot** see the computer screen. If the SME watches the screen, his or her attention may be diverted from identifying relevant content to pointing out typing errors.

While setting up the computer and arranging the work area, chat with the SME to develop rapport. Once the work area is set up, tell the SME that you will:
- first explain the training program
- next, discuss the interviewing process
- then, plan the work and get started

Interviewing to Gather Relevant Content for Training

Major Step 2—Explain the Training Program

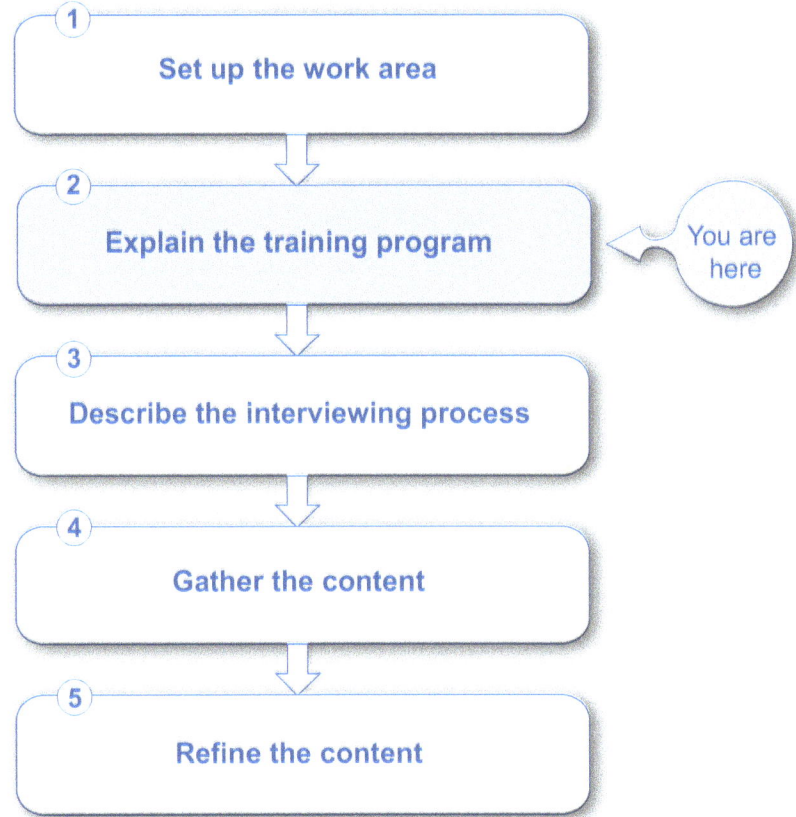

For an SME to be effective in providing information, he or she must have an understanding of the training program, including:
- purpose and importance of the training program
- training design materials such as a training profile or program outline and scope document (if available)
- methods of delivering and administering training
- features of the training resource (e.g., self-instructional modules)

Ask the SME if the training program has been explained to him/her. The SME may have had some previous exposure to the training program:
- The SME may have been a participant during the sessions to develop the training profile or program outline and has a good understanding of the program scope and training

PART B Section 6
Conducting the Interview

program benefits. The SME may also have a partial understanding of how the training will be delivered and administered.
- The SME may have attended a group meeting in which you or your team leader made a presentation on the training program and its benefits.
- For large training programs, the training may be implemented before all of the resources are developed. In this case, the SME may have been given a formal explanation of the training program and may already have used some of the training resources.

If the SME has had some exposure to the training program, find out what he or she knows, and then explain the topics that have not been discussed. If the SME has had little exposure to the training program, show the training design material and give a brief explanation of the:
- training profile/program outline
- scope document or expanded table of contents
- finished product (e.g., training module)

Refer to Part 2 of Attachment 3—*Interviewing Checklist* for a detailed explanation of each topic.

You must make sure the SME is familiar with **all** the information listed in Part 2 of Attachment 3—*Interviewing Checklist*. If one or more items are missed, misunderstandings can occur. You and the customer will then have to make a special effort to correct the misunderstandings and persuade employees to accept the training program.

Use Part 2 of Attachment 3—*Interviewing Checklist* as a job aid for explaining the training program.

Explaining the features of the training resources to be developed (e.g., a module) helps the SME understand the type of content and the level of detail that he or she must provide. After you have completed your explanation, ask the SME if he or she has any questions about the design of the training program.

The SME may have some concerns about staff layoffs: *If training makes employees and the organization more efficient, won't that reduce the need for staff, resulting in layoffs?*

Your response depends on the customer's purposes for developing the training. If you do not know whether the training could lead to layoffs, say so. You can still make some positive responses like the ones listed below. From the following suggestions, select the responses that match the objectives of your customer's training program and corporate goals.

1. **For most customers, training will not result in layoffs.**
   - Through training, employees can do their jobs better, more efficiently, and more safely. However, the position still needs to be filled because the work cannot be redesigned to reduce staff (e.g., an employee can only drive to thirty oil wells in a day. Being safer and more effective at monitoring each well does not reduce the travel time).
   - Often, the training is tied to career development and progression schemes. As an employee receives training and moves up the progression ladder, his or her vacated position must be filled.
   - Employees who do not wish to progress can remain in their positions, provided they complete the minimum training.
   - Training can be designed to give the organization a more flexible work force. Employees may change jobs but the jobs do not disappear.
   - The training program may be part of a plan to expand the work force.

2. **Training can sometimes lead to staff reductions.**
   Training can be part of the plan to redesign the work so that employees have expanded roles. The redesign of the work could result in a major improvement in efficiency and, consequently, a reduction in staffing. (For example,

traditionally, two people, an operator and a maintenance person, had to drive to a pipeline station to do repairs. After training, only one person had to drive to the station because he or she could now maintain and operate the station.) Training employees to use new, more efficient technology could also lead to a reduction in staff.

Generally, you should emphasize the positive benefits of training to downplay the concerns about layoffs, unless the customer has stated that one of the purposes of training is to reduce the size of the staff. Even if there is a possibility of layoffs, employees can reduce the risk of being laid off by demonstrating an interest in completing the training. Here are some possible responses to the SME in the event that some staff could be laid off:

- Organizations who invest in training staff want to retain them.
- Organizations want to retain employees who show interest in improving their personal abilities and in making the organization a success.
- The staff could be downsized through attrition or by placement of employees in a different part of the organization.
- An ineffective employee who does not try to improve his or her performance could be laid off. (This statement could be true even if there is no training program.)

Major Step 3—Describe the Interviewing Process

Before gathering content, explain the interviewing process to the SME so he or she has an understanding of the interviewing process and his or her roles and responsibilities. Key topics that must be explained include the following:
- strength of the interviewing process
- procedure for identifying and recording information
- description of the format used to document information
- refinement and validation of the content (quality control)
- establishment of relevant content criteria

 Interviewing to Gather Relevant Content for Training

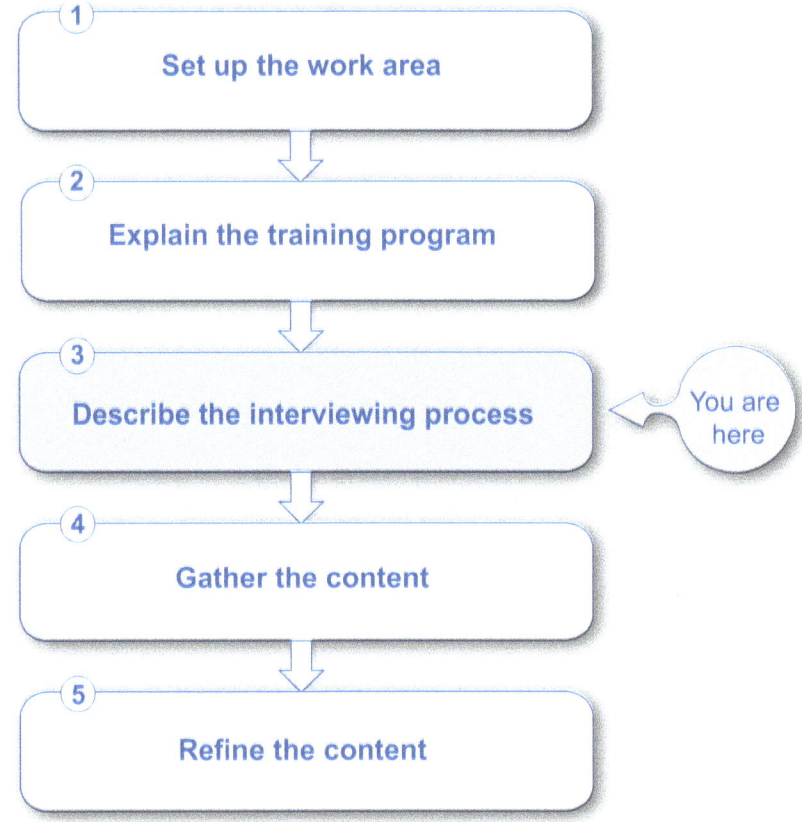

Part 2 of Attachment 3—*Interviewing Checklist* lists specific points for topics that you should explain to the SME. Key issues associated with the topics include:

Benefits of the interviewing process—If the SME has not provided content before, he or she may be a bit apprehensive and uncertain. The SME may not understand what has to be done, how the work will be carried out, or how the work will impact his or her personal credibility. Reassure the SME by telling him or her that the two of you will work cooperatively to identify the required content. Tell him or her that the interviewing process is the best of two worlds. As a training/writing expert, you have the training/educational expertise and will provide direction to ensure that the right types of content are identified and organized. Tell the SME that he or she knows the company and the job the best, and will be able to provide the specific information that will be used in the training materials.

PART B Section 6
Conducting the Interview

 If you have technical expertise or experience in the field for which you are developing training, downplay your qualifications. It is recommended that you do not tell the SME of your technical qualifications for two reasons:
- the SME may be intimidated and reluctant to provide information in case it is not correct
- you may provide specific information or work strategies that do not match the site's expectations

By appearing to be less knowledgeable about the content than you probably are, you can be a better listener and ask more comprehensive questions. This strategy will enable you to get quality information that matches the customer's expectations and context, and avoid *telling* the customer how to do the job.

Identifying and recording information—Tell the SME that you will direct the interview by asking a lot of questions and will type the information he or she gives you on the computer.

Describing the format for recording information—There are many different formats that can be used to record the information gathered from the SME.

Show an example of the format you use for gathering content and explain the key features. Make sure to tell the SME that his or her name is recorded in the header so that you and others will know who to contact if there are further questions. Make it clear that the finished training resource will not include names.

 The format has both educational and module design attributes:
- *educational* because the content is stated as training and performance behaviors (audience, conditions, performance, and standards)
- *module design* because the content is grouped and sequenced

127

Interviewing to Gather Relevant Content for Training

NOTE — Putting the SME's name on the document gives that person recognition for his or her contributions to the training program and a sense of both responsibility and accomplishment.

Refining and validating the content (quality control)—Tell the SME that during the interview some information may be missed because that's the nature of conducting interviews. Tell the SME that you will review the content that is gathered and may need to ask him or her for further clarification. If you are meeting with the SME for consecutive days, it is recommended that in the evenings, you review the content you have gathered.

When reviewing the content:
- identify errors and omissions
- reword your information more clearly
- re-sequence information and make sure the content is correctly organized by level of detail

At the following meeting, you can ask the SME to help fill in omissions and clarify content.

After you have refined the content, the SME may want to review a paper copy to ensure the information is accurate and complete.

NOTE — Depending on the customer, both the gathered content *and* the training material, or the training material only, will be validated by several of the customer's staff.

Establishing criteria for relevant content—Identifying the required content and the level of detail can be difficult. All kinds of training could be developed but it is important to limit the training so that it is relevant, useful, and practical. The training must contribute to employee, job, and corporate performance. You need to apply many of the thinking strategies identified in Part A while interviewing to ensure relevant content is gathered. A very powerful strategy you can use is to get the SME's approval as to the key criteria for relevant content.

The following illustration shows a practical way to present key criteria for relevant content to the SME. Print and show a customized list similar to the one that follows.

Criteria for Relevant Content	
Application	Corporate Objectives
Decisions Tasks	• safety • environment • legislation • equipment reliability and life • equipment optimization • energy use • quality • loss control • cost control • customer satisfaction • public image • public disruption • reputation • communication • teamwork

IMPORTANT

The criteria for relevant content vary between projects, depending on the purpose of the resources being developed and the customer's goals. Make sure you understand the criteria for relevant content for your project before interviewing the SME. Always keep in mind that all of the training must begin and end in a **job application—people performing tasks and making decisions**.

After showing the SME the list of criteria, tell the SME that:
- Criteria are used to identify training content.
- For training to be relevant, it must help the trainee do tasks and *make effective decisions*.
- The *corporate objectives* define what is important for training. After gathering content, checking the corporate objectives helps determine whether all important content has been identified.

- The criteria help decide if specific content should be included or left out. Not all tasks and knowledge are of equal importance:
  - if the knowledge or task affects the corporate objectives, then that content should be included in the training.
  - if the knowledge or task does **not** have an impact on the corporate objectives, then the content should not be included in the training.

NOTE

During the interview, there is a possibility that you and the SME may disagree about whether specific content should be included or excluded. Using written criteria as a means of making decisions about the content makes decision making more objective, minimizing the potential for developing personal conflicts between you and the SME. Getting the SME's agreement on the criteria for relevant content at the beginning of the interview helps persuade the SME to use these criteria for decision making.

Make sure the list of relevant content criteria is visible to the SME and other customer staff who may be present.

In addition to using the above relevant content criteria about tasks, decisions, and corporate goals, you need to apply many other thinking strategies introduced in Part A. When applying the thinking strategies, first ask yourself the questions. Next, if you think the questions are relevant, ask the SME.

Describe the interviewing process

Preparing the SME for the interviewing process contributes to the efficiency of the interview to identify relevant, useful, and practical content.

The following questions apply to normal conditions unless otherwise stated. From the given choices, select the best answer to each question. Although other choices may apply under different conditions, do not consider these choices as being the best answers.

PART B Section 6
Conducting the Interview

1. Whenever possible, interviewing should take place in the office of the SME's supervisor.

    a. true
    b. false

2. Before starting a content-gathering interview, you must ensure that the SME has an understanding of the _____.

    a. purpose and importance of the training program
    b. training profile or program outline and scope document
    c. methods of delivering and administering training
    d. features of the training materials
    e. all of the above

3. If the SME or another employee expresses a concern that the training may result in staff layoffs, you should _____.

    a. refuse to discuss the issue
    b. minimize the negative impact that the training could have on individual employees
    c. tell the employee that the workforce will not be reduced, even if there is a good possibility of a reduction
    d. tell the employee that, after the training program is developed, anyone **not** interested in improving his or her abilities will be laid off

4. The main strength(s) of the interviewing process is that it _____.

    a. uses your and the SME's respective expertise to develop training materials
    b. is the fastest way to collect relevant content for training material development
    c. is a means of improving the SME's communication skills
    d. all of the above

5. If you have technical expertise in a field for which you are developing training, you should downplay your qualifications when interviewing SMEs.

   a. true
   b. false

6. You should explain the criteria for gathering relevant content and the benefits of using the criteria to identify content.

   a. true
   b. false

7. The relevant content criteria are used to _____.

   a. identify training content
   b. check if all important content has been identified
   c. help decide whether specific content should be included or excluded
   d. all of the above

Answer Key
1. b
2. e
3. b
4. a
5. a
6. a
7. d

Major Step 4—Gather the Content

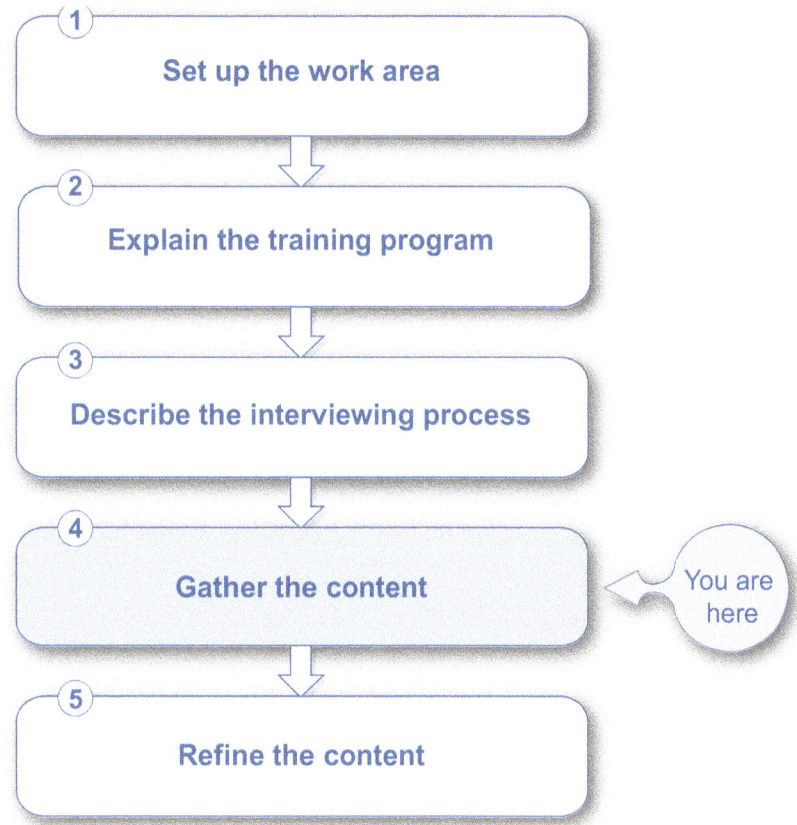

To provide leadership to gather the content, follow these five sub-steps:

Sub-step 1—Select the first competency to work on

Sub-step 2—Identify the audience and training sequence

Sub-step 3—Identify the job applications

Sub-step 4—Develop the topic outline

Sub-step 5—Gather and record relevant content

Interviewing to Gather Relevant Content for Training

Sub-step 1—Select the first competency to work on

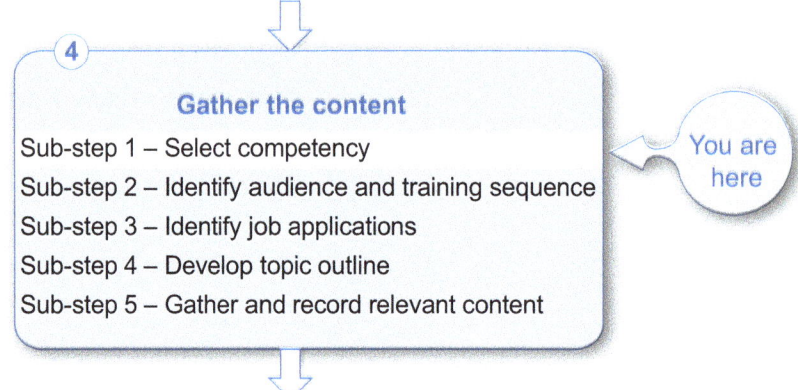

Content may have to be gathered for several competencies or program objectives. You need to plan a content-gathering sequence that meets both your and the SME's needs.

Your Needs

You may have to gather content on a topic about which you have only a basic understanding (a common and challenging situation). You must learn both the generalities and specifics of the technology, processes, tasks, and administration system. Much of this learning takes place while gathering the content for the training program. Plan the *content-gathering* sequence to complement your personal understanding of the required content and your learning preference (e.g., general to specific, or specific to general). The assumption is that you will develop the training resources in the same order that you are using or used to gather the content. (For large projects, content gathering and training resource development will be staggered.)

Here are three common training module development sequencing scenarios and their related challenges. In the explanations, the term *self-instructional module* is used. The scenarios presented below use the term *competency* and *self-instructional module* by way of explanation. The design of self-instructional modules can vary and often has features such as: competency title and reference number, table of contents, list of training objectives, self-instruction, and self test. A knowledge test may also be developed.

PART B Section 6
Conducting the Interview

Scenario 1

An oil and gas company is developing a training program for their field and gas plant operators. You will be developing self-instructional training modules for two competencies:

- Module AA—*Describe Company Facilities* will give a new trainee an overview of the company's field and gas plant facilities. The purpose of the module will be to orient the trainee to the company's facilities. The module will give a description of the buildings and their locations, specify the raw and refined products, and identify the refining processes. The module will also address basic safety issues.

- Module FF—*Describe Field Compressors* will provide the trainee with advanced training. For each compressor application, the trainee must be able to describe the principles of operation, the equipment and its functions, and identify the variables that must be monitored and adjusted. Safety, loss control, and optimization will be emphasized throughout the module.

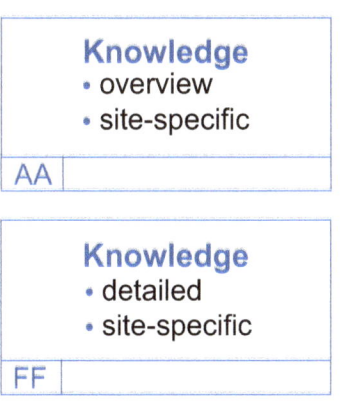

If you choose to develop Module AA first, you need to know the generalities and some of the specifics in order to determine which content belongs in Module AA and which content belongs in Module FF. If you choose to gather content for Module AA first, you may fall into the trap of gathering content that is much too detailed. Some of the content will then have to be transferred to more advanced modules. To limit the content for module AA, you must have a clear understanding of the goals or outcomes the module is to achieve.

If you choose to gather the content for Module FF first, you may not yet have a general understanding of the company, the technology, or the operation. Without this general knowledge, you may have difficulty gathering content that fits the customer's context.

Interviewing to Gather Relevant Content for Training

Based on your personal knowledge, experience, and learning style, you need to decide which sequence will work best for you and gather content in that order.

Scenario 2

A pulp company is developing a training program for its mill operators. You will be developing self-instructional modules for twelve competencies:

- Module 01—*Describe the Paper Making Process* will give a new trainee an overview of the company's mill and manufacturing processes. The purpose of the module will be to orient the trainee to the company and the technology. It will prepare the trainee for learning specific tasks. The module will describe the buildings and their locations, specify the raw and refined products, explain the manufacturing processes, and identify the operator's roles and responsibilities.

- Modules 02 to 12—*Describe and Carry out Tasks* (a, b, c, etc....) will provide advanced training in performing specific tasks. A separate module addressing the task and support knowledge will be developed for each task. The sequencing of the modules for training has been determined according to the technology, the job cycle, and the complexity of the tasks.

Knowledge • overview • site-specific	**Knowledge and Task**	**Task**
01	02	03
Task	**Knowledge and Task**	**Task**
04	05	06

Each advanced module will require the trainee to be able to describe the principles of operation, the equipment and its function(s), identify the variables that must be monitored and adjusted, and perform a specific task. Safety, loss control, and optimization will be emphasized throughout each module. The trainee will receive specific on-the-job coaching.

To demonstrate competence, the trainee will have to answer all the knowledge check questions (written test) correctly and perform the task to a specific standard.

If you prefer to learn from the general to the specific, develop the modules in the order in which they appear on the training profile/outline to get a sense of the sequence of learning. Developing Module 01 first gives you a general understanding of the technology, tasks, and decision-making issues. However, developing Module 01 first requires you to have a clear understanding of the goals or outcomes of the module as well as an understanding of the specifics to be addressed in the advanced modules. Your challenge is to develop Module 01 so that it will provide an overview to prepare the trainee for advanced training and, at the same time, limit the amount of content repeated in the advanced modules.

If you prefer to learn from the specific to the general, you may find it easier to develop the specific task-focused modules first and then develop the introduction/overview module. While gathering content, you must always keep in mind the content that belongs in other modules as well as the training sequence.

Scenario 3

One of the more complex training program designs includes generic training required to carry out tasks. A good example is a training program for pipeline Control Centre Operators (CCOs). In this scenario, you will develop modules for three types of competencies:

- Module 07—*Describe Pipelines* will provide an overview of the pipelines, their configurations, types, and throughput of products, and describe the CCO's roles and responsibilities.
- Modules 21 to 28 will describe the control centre computer systems and screens. Some modules will also specify the computer procedures operators use to monitor, control, and troubleshoot the pipelines. The knowledge and skills gained from these modules will be a means to an end; the trainee will first learn to operate the computers and then learn to operate specific pipelines. An alternative training design is to have the trainee concurrently learn to operate

the computers and the pipelines. However, it is usually more efficient to train CCOs to use the computers first and then have them learn to operate the pipelines. Learning to use the computers first limits the complexity of the pipeline operating procedures by eliminating the need to specify computer operations at the same time.

- Modules 41 to 49 will have an introductory module which gives an overview of the pipeline system followed by modules that focus on tasks (in this case, operating a specific pipeline).

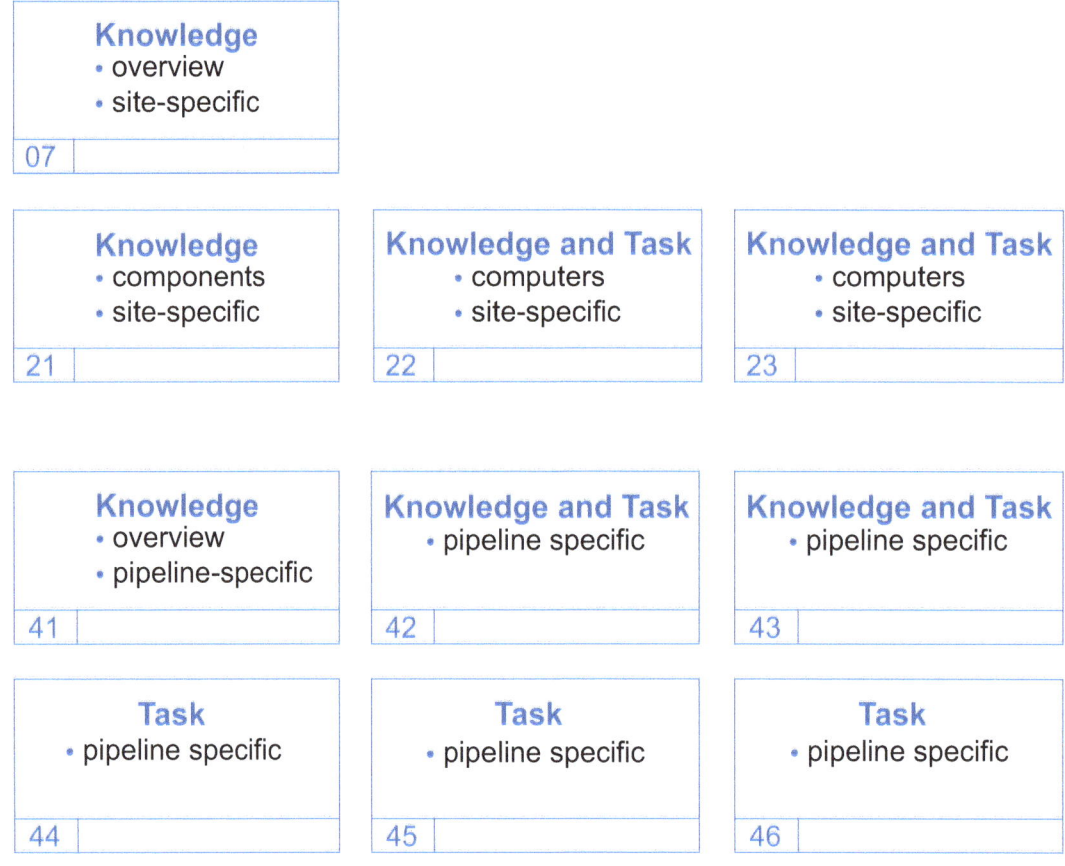

You could start gathering content on any module. When deciding where to start, consider your experience with the content and your personal learning style. While gathering content, you must always keep in mind the content that belongs in other modules as well as the training sequence.

PART B Section 6
Conducting the Interview

SME's Needs

The SME may have several concerns such as:
- his or her comfort with the content needed for the modules. For example, the SME may feel uncertain about providing content if he or she has **not** done that type of work for more than a year.
- personal likes or dislikes for the specific technology, processes, or tasks
- ability to provide the content in some logical order (e.g., following the training sequence, following the technology design)
- uncertainty as to your expectations for providing content; the SME may want to start with an easy module
- availability of related documentation

Through discussion, you and the SME should plan a content-gathering sequence that meets both your needs. A good way to start planning is to ask the SME which competency he or she would like to work on first.

Sub-step 2—Identify the audience and training sequence

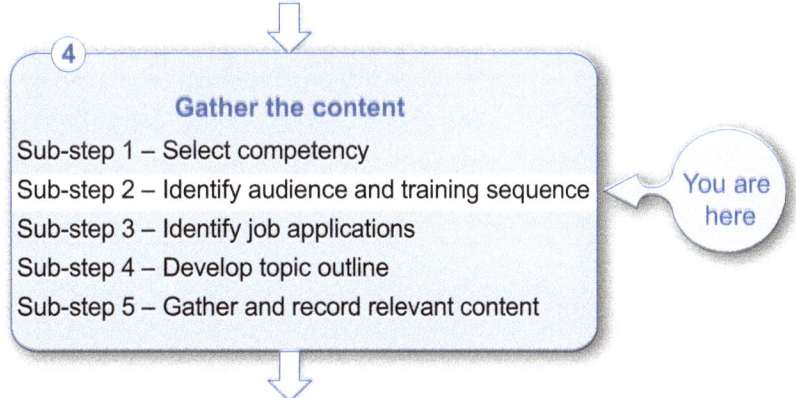

Having selected a competency to work on, you and the SME must develop a common understanding of the relationship of the specific training to the overall training program so that you can gather content relevant to that competency. Discuss the following points with the SME:
- intended audience
- education level of current and future trainees
- specialized external training requirements (e.g., apprentice, journeyman, vendor training)

139

Interviewing to Gather Relevant Content for Training

- experience in the present position (new, intermediate, advanced)

NOTE Some modules may be developed for two or more audiences. Before gathering content, define all audiences that will use the training.

- sequence of training
  - type of training outcomes (knowledge, tasks, or both). The verb(s) used in the competency statement, as well as the information provided in the scope document, suggest the types of learning outcomes and possible method(s) of evaluation (knowledge and/or on-the-job performance).
  - relationship of the competency to prerequisite and advanced competencies
  - related competencies
  - relationship of the competency to production requirements (people given work assignments based on production requirements, staffing changes, and vacations may affect the sequence for gathering content). Your customer may ask you to develop the training that meets its immediate training needs first.

By identifying the level of training, sequence, and intent of the training, you and the SME will develop a general idea of the relationships between the competency, the overall program, and the job. This knowledge helps you and the SME understand the scope of the training and reduces overlaps and omissions.

Sub-step 3—Identify the job applications

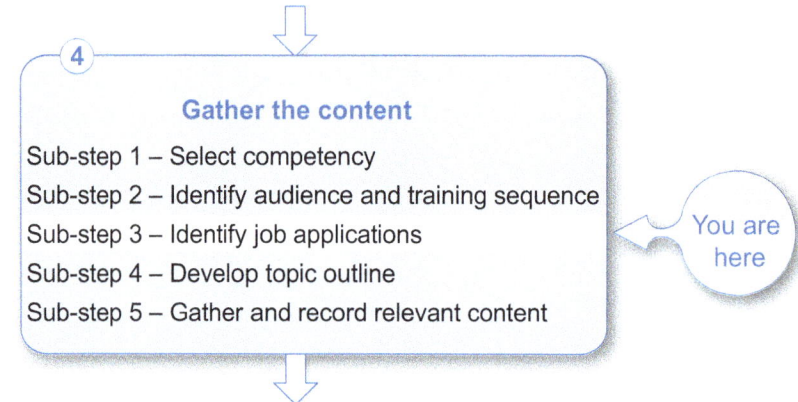

PART B Section 6
Conducting the Interview

This sub-step deals with the specifics of training for the selected competency. Before gathering content, you and the SME must develop a common understanding of the purpose and specific training requirements of the competency, including:
- job applications of the training. Training must culminate in a job application (task) and/or help the trainee make decisions. Remember, training is **not** provided for all the tasks that the trainee must perform.
- type, scope, and desired detail of the content

The type and detail of information you must gather depends on the training that the module addresses:
- performance
- performance and knowledge, or
- knowledge

Ask the SME how he or she would know that the trainee is competent. For example, *Should the trainee complete a knowledge test and/or perform tasks on the job as a demonstration of competence?*

The answer to your question helps the SME to understand the intent and focus of the training.

Modules which address either performance or performance and knowledge

If the training requires the trainee to perform a specific task, you and your SME must discuss the task in considerable detail before gathering the content. Answers to the following types of question will help you to understand what is involved:
- *What task must the trainee perform?*
- *How often must the task be performed?*
- *What are the pre-conditions that require the task to be performed?*
- *Under what conditions must the task be performed?*
- *How difficult is it to carry out the task?*
- *What are the major steps in carrying out the task?*
- *Are there any critical issues when performing the task that can affect people, equipment, materials, environment, or the organization (PEMEO)?*
- *How well must the task be performed?*

Interviewing to Gather Relevant Content for Training

- *How do you know the task is performed satisfactorily (i.e., what are the indicators of performance)?*
- *What are the consequences if the task is **not** completed, or if the task is **not** completed satisfactorily?*

This understanding about the task also helps you and the SME to:
- determine whether the trainee requires support knowledge to do the task safely and effectively
- identify the support knowledge (if required)

Modules which address knowledge only

If the training requires the trainee to acquire knowledge only, your major concern is to identify module content that is practical, useful, and contributes to the customer's corporate goals. You must make sure that the training provided by the knowledge-based module (possibly in conjunction with other related modules) culminates in a job application (performing tasks effectively) and/or contributes to decision making. Working with the SME, identify the tasks where the knowledge is needed to work safely and effectively.

If the module applies to an introductory/overview competency such as *Describe Paper Making Process*, the tasks to which the knowledge applies are relatively easy to identify. Check the training profile or program outline for competencies listed in the same group (topic) that focus on tasks.

If the module addresses generic knowledge, identifying the tasks to which the knowledge applies is more difficult. Often, generic training relates to several tasks. The tasks may be randomly listed throughout the training profile or program outline. Some related tasks may not be listed. Sometimes a generic module is a prerequisite for a more advanced knowledge-based module. In that case, examine the advanced knowledge-based module to determine the tasks to which the advanced module applies.

Once you have identified the tasks that relate to the knowledge-based module, you need to learn more about the tasks to identify critical knowledge that must be gathered.

PART B Section 6
Conducting the Interview

Use the list of questions for modules that are task-focused (see page 141) to gain an understanding about the tasks.

Make sure that you record the tasks to which the knowledge-based module applies. This list of tasks will help you to limit the content for the knowledge-based module to useful applications. When you write the module, you will be able to use this list of tasks to provide practical examples of the knowledge being applied to the job.

Using application examples makes the knowledge more meaningful for the trainee and emphasizes the importance of learning the content.

Summary: Sub-step 3

At this point in the interview process, you have accomplished several important goals:
- established the criteria for selecting relevant content
- selected a competency for which content will be gathered
- identified the qualifications of the target audience including education, job experience, internal training, and external training that has been completed
- within the training program, identified the training sequence (pre- and post-requisites) for the competency that you are going to work on
- identified other competencies related to the one you are going to work on
- identified practical job applications for the competency as well as some of the critical issues associated with the tasks.

You and the SME now have a general understanding of the focus, scope, and purpose of the training module. You have also helped the SME understand the general issues and information that the training should address. You will now help the SME organize his or her thoughts by completing the next sub-step of the content-gathering process (Develop topic outline).

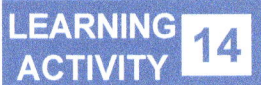

Interviewing to Gather Relevant Content for Training

LEARNING ACTIVITY 14

Identify the first competency to work on, the training sequence, and outcomes

Identifying the first training competency for which to gather content, the training sequence, and the training outcomes helps you and the SME identify specific content that is relevant, useful, and practical.

The following questions apply to normal conditions unless otherwise stated. From the given choices, select the best answer to each question. Although other choices may apply under different conditions, do not consider these choices as being the best answers.

1. If the SME seems to have some difficulties providing relevant content, you should _____.

    a. ask the site supervisor to provide a different SME
    b. compensate by asking pertinent questions
    c. discuss the problem with your project leader
    d. start the interviewing process over again
    e. any of the above

2. Selection of the first competency to work on is dependent upon _____.

    a. the SME's personal preference
    b. your personal preference
    c. both yours and the SME's needs
    d. the design of the customer's training program

3. When selecting the first competency for gathering content, keep in mind _____.

    a. the content that belongs in other modules
    b. the training sequence
    c. the training administration system
    d. all of the above
    e. a and b only
    f. a and c only

PART B Section 6
Conducting the Interview

4. After selecting a competency to work on, you and the SME should then _____.

   a. identify the job applications
   b. develop the topic outline
   c. identify the audience and training sequence
   d. gather and record relevant content

5. The type of training outcomes and possible method(s) of evaluation for a competency are often indicated by the verb(s) used in the competency statement.

   a. true
   b. false

6. For training to be useful to a customer, the training must culminate in a job application. A job application is defined by the _____.

   a. tasks performed by employees
   b. decisions made by employees
   c. corporate mission statement
   d. a and b
   e. b and c

7. For a module addressing generic knowledge, tasks to which the module applies may be identified _____.

   a. throughout the customer's training profile or program outline
   b. in a more advanced module
   c. through discussion with the SME
   d. all of the above

Answer Key
1. b
2. c
3. e
4. c
5. a
6. d
7. d

Sub-step 4—Develop the topic outline

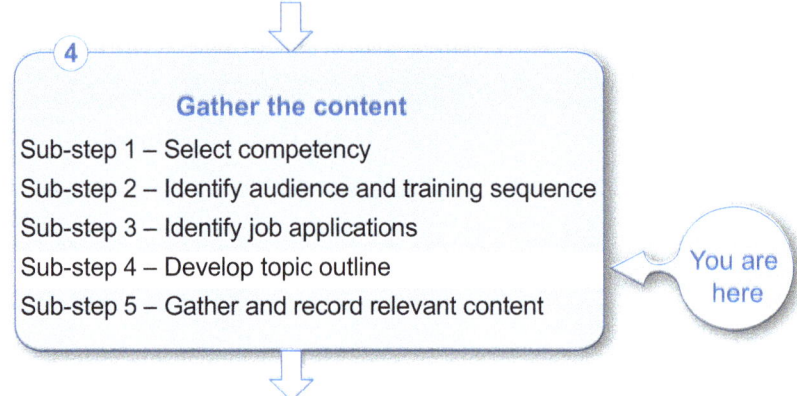

Developing a topic outline for the module has several important benefits:
- formalizes the type of content that will be addressed in the module
- organizes the SME's thoughts and yours (grouping and sequencing ideas)
- structures and sequences the content for the written resource
- provides a basis for identifying and sequencing some of the training objectives

 You must develop a topic outline before gathering specific content to ensure the efficient development of quality resources.

A basic topic outline can be equivalent to the section titles for a module, for example:

1. The content for a module which describes a process flow would probably be structured in the same sequence as the process such as:
   - raw material inlet distribution
   - raw material refining
   - raw material separation
   - etc.

2. The content for a module about operating a portable electronic measuring device can be structured as follows:
   - principles of operation

- components and their function
- alarms and readings
- equipment controls
- etc.

Until now, the SME has answered questions relating to the type of training that will be developed. By discussing the topic outline you are now asking the SME to begin focusing on the content. An excellent way to initiate discussion about the topic outline is to say to the SME, *Before we begin, tell me about the technology (or process, or task).* Casually lean back in your chair and relax. This action will put the SME at ease. You are giving the SME an opportunity to informally experience providing information (i.e., you are using the guided discovery training method to introduce the SME to the content-gathering process).

As the SME gives the description, listen closely to identify the main topics and to determine the order in which the topics could be sequenced. You may want to jot down key words. For some SMEs, you will have to provide additional prompts, such as:
- *What are the main components of the process?*
- *What are the major steps for completing the task?*

After the SME has completed the description and answered your general questions, suggest an outline of the topics for the module. Either write the topics in point form or create a flow diagram of the topics. It is usually best **not** to include the *Introduction* as one of the topics in the outline at this time. The SME is probably thinking in terms of the job and the technology, and not in terms of providing effective instruction—the introduction's primary purpose is to prepare the trainee for learning. *Confirm* with the SME that the outline identifies what is required for the module. For example, ask, *If we divided the content into these topics, would it work for training?*

Throughout the interviewing process, confirm with the SME that the information you gather is correct, accurate, and is needed for training. The confirmation process reduces the potential for misunderstandings and demonstrates that you are committed to doing your best for your customer.

Interviewing to Gather Relevant Content for Training

After you and the SME agree on the topic outline, indicate that an introduction is also required. Although it is possible to leave development of the introduction to when you are writing the training resources, there are several benefits of getting the SME to help with the introduction:

- You may have difficulty identifying the content for the introduction, such as:
  - the big picture
  - definitions
  - purpose
  - importance
- You may have difficulty wording the introduction in a way that fits the customer's context.
- You can save a lot of time and effort. Writing introductions can be difficult.
- You and the SME get a better understanding of the purpose and importance of the training.

Once you have developed the topic outline, you may want to expand the outline into an expanded scope (often called a module outline for content gathering). Attachment 4 is an example of a module outline for content gathering. You may want to create the module outline for gathering content on the computer and print a copy. Refer to the relevant content criteria to ensure that there are no omissions of important content. If you or the SME have concerns that information may be missed, you may be able to get other customer staff to validate the outline. If others are to validate the outline, make sure that at the top of the page you identify the **audience** and the **job tasks** to which the training relates. If it is not necessary or not possible to have the outline validated immediately, either continue to gather content for the competency, or develop outlines for other competencies.

NOTE Sometimes a module outline for content gathering is developed and validated before conducting the interview. Review the outline with the SME and get his or her approval before proceeding with the interview.

Sometimes a committee develops the scope or content outline of a module/competency. If you and the SME decide to add or delete content, make sure you inform all committee members of major changes and get their approval.

Develop topic outline

Developing a topic outline is an important activity for both the SME and you to complete before gathering specific content.

The following questions apply to normal conditions unless otherwise stated. From the given choices, select the best answer to each question. Although other choices may apply under different conditions, do not consider these choices as being the best answers.

1. As part of the interviewing process, developing a topic outline for a module is beneficial because the topic outline _____.

   a. formalizes the type of content to be addressed
   b. organizes the SME's thoughts
   c. structures and sequences the content for the module
   d. provides a basis for developing training objectives
   e. all of the above

2. Developing a topic outline before gathering specific content makes writing the training module more efficient.

   a. true
   b. false

Answer Key

1. e
2. a

Sub-step 5—Gather and record relevant content

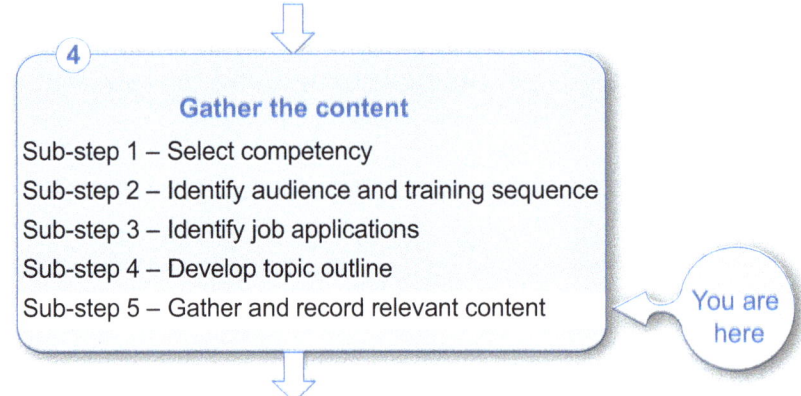

Up to this point in the interview process, you have provided a great deal of leadership in working with the SME to:
- identify general training outcomes for a competency, and
- determine the type of content required for the module

To carry out Sub-step 5 of the interviewing process, you must continue to provide leadership to ensure the content being gathered is relevant, accurate, specific, and complete. **Throughout this step, you must continually search for missing content and question yourself as to the accuracy of the information that the SME provides.** You can use several thinking strategies explained in Part A to ensure you do a competent job gathering relevant content.

1. Always keep in mind the key goals you are working towards:
   - the purpose of the module (the training outcomes that the module must address)
   - efficient instruction (ease of learning—developmental, specific, accurate, complete)
   - your need to be efficient at gathering content by:
     – reducing the need to return to the site to gather missing content
     – gathering only necessary detail
   - efficiency in writing the module and producing a quality product

2. Refer to the topic outline to ensure that you are gathering the right type of content and that the content is sequenced developmentally and logically.

PART B   Section 6
Conducting the Interview

3. Refer to the criteria for relevant content to identify types of content that should be included in the module. Then, after gathering a chunk of content, refer to the criteria again to ensure specific types of content have not been forgotten or overlooked.

4. Apply LO-PEMEO (Loss, Optimization–People, Equipment, Materials, Environment, Organization) to identify important content.

NOTE Although some domains of LO-PEMEO may not appear to apply to a situation (e.g., safety in an office environment), consider the possibility that the domain could apply to eliminate any doubts.

5. While gathering the content, examine the performance and training from different points of view.

Position	Some Perspectives
Trainee	• concerned about own safety and safety of others • concerned about causing damage to equipment and products (possibly being reprimanded) • wonders what to do if things are not as expected (decision making) • stressed from learning a new job and administrative protocols • wants to meet supervisor's or team's approval
Coach	• concerned for trainee's safety • does not want to disrupt work while training • concerned about being effective in providing instruction (instructional process and communication) • concerned that the trainee learns to do the work effectively and can make good decisions (needs proof) **Note:** A self-instructional module serves as a coach in that the module performs a coaching/teaching function.

(continued)

Position	Some Perspectives
Supervisor or team	• concerned that the trainee does not get hurt or does not hurt others • concerned that the trainee does not downgrade the operation • concerned that the trainee understands company goals and contributes to these goals • concerned that the trainee meets work standards • wants the trainee to be productive in the shortest time possible • wants the trainee to learn and follow administrative and management protocols • wants the trainee to make good decisions
Consultant Technical writer (you)	• wants to help the trainee to be a productive employee • concerned that the training is practical, effective, and efficient • concerned that there are no incorrect instructions, errors, or omissions that could put people at risk or downgrade the customer's operation • concerned that the training resources meet the customer's approval • concerned that there is enough specific information for him/herself or another consultant to be able to write the module • concerned that the information gathered will make writing the module easy and efficient

6. While gathering the content, question yourself as to the implications of the information (reasons, causes, effects, consequences, *what if...* it doesn't work, it behaves differently, or a variable is changed?). Having asked yourself these types of question, you can eliminate many of the questions as **not** being important, and then ask the SME the relevant questions.

7. Identify the variables (e.g., temperature, rpm, throughput, number of customers, number of complaints) that relate

to the technology or process. Ask yourself, and in some cases ask the SME, questions relating to the variables, for example:
- *What can cause the variable to change?*
- *What happens when the variable changes?*
- *What is the acceptable range or set point for the variable?*
- *What should the worker do if the variable changes?*
- *Why would the worker want to change the variable?*
- *Does the worker have control over the variable?*
- *Does the worker have the authority to change the variable?*
- *How does the worker change the variable?*
- *What is the impact on PEMEO if the variable is/is not changed?*

Using customer resources for information

To develop effective instruction, try to identify examples, possible analogies and graphics that can be used in the module. Get resources from the SME that will help you understand the content or help you write the module. These resources may include the following:
- graphics
- maps
- charts
- computer printouts
- Piping and Instrumentation Drawings (P&IDs)
- hand-drawn sketches
- equipment and operating specifications

To eliminate any confusion that might surface when you are developing the training module, put the module numbers on all of the above resources. Distinct labeling is particularly important if the resources apply to more than one module. Make sure all graphics are drawn accurately and labeled clearly. Do not abbreviate labels on graphics because others on your team may have to use the information you have gathered to write the module and may not understand your coding.

If you are going to reference specific customer resources such as an emergency response manual, make notes in the computer file to indicate the specific name and pages that are to be referenced. Manuals and written resources that are on loan from the customer must also be labeled (company, location, person) and promptly returned when they are no longer needed.

Sometimes the information you require may be recorded in one of the customer's manuals. However, do not accept the SME's word that the information you require is adequately explained in the manual. Review the manual yourself to ensure that the content is current, accurate, and provides the specific information you require.

The content-gathering and recording process

The following explanation makes suggestions for gathering content and also identifies some pitfalls. The content-gathering process outlined below is used as a means to identify specific issues; the intent is not to provide a specific process. As you read the explanation, you can determine for yourself which suggestions would help you.

There are many different style sheets that can be used to record content. Some style sheets are formatted to have a strong emphasis on applying training concepts; others are formatted to make it easy to record the content, especially for knowledge competencies.

If a style sheet that makes it easy to record content is used, the focus on training can either get de-emphasized or dropped. The danger then is that the focus shifts from people to content. Unnecessary content may be recorded and content important to employee performance missed. If conditions (e.g., given normal conditions, given emergency conditions) are not specified, the content you gather could be off the topic.

The style sheet may include stating the training objectives. The training objectives help keep the goals in mind while gathering the content. If training objectives are not part of the style sheet, you should consider recording the key descriptors as part of the content for the topics (refer to Section 2.6—*Work Effectively*). For example:
- audience
- preconditions

- conditions
- performance
- standards

Show the SME an example of a finished content-gathering style sheet (from another project). Make sure the other customer has approved you showing the content so that you are not breaching confidentiality. Explain the main features. Tell the SME that you will be recording the information in point form. When you develop the training module, you will write the content in paragraphs, include illustrations, and use educational concepts to improve comprehension and long-term retention of the information.

Begin by calling up the style sheet on the computer and naming the file. Fill in the information in the header to ensure you have information about the SME. Either ask the SME for the correct spelling of his or her name, or repeat the person's name to remind the SME of the importance of his or her involvement.

If procedures must be developed for several tasks, experienced consultants will sometimes use the customer's style sheet for procedures and immediately produce a rough draft of the final product.

Always save your computer file regularly to prevent loss of data should the computer fail or you accidentally delete information. You may want to use the *Auto-Save* or the *Reminder to Save* features if you tend to forget to manually save your work. Auto-Save has the disadvantage of potentially saving at inappropriate times.

Also, make frequent backup copies on your external memory device.

You are now ready to identify the specific knowledge the trainee must acquire and specify the actions the trainee must demonstrate to prove competence. On the style sheet, use the performance statements or topic headings to organize and record the content.

It is recommended that you start by gathering content for the introduction. Make sure you identify the purpose and importance of the task or technology.

The *purpose* of a task is to achieve a specific result. The purpose of technology is to perform a function. When determining the purpose of the technology, be specific, especially if you are gathering content for an application of the technology. For example, a pump transfers liquids.
- *What type of liquid is being transferred?*
- *The liquid is transferred from where to where?*

Make sure you discuss the importance of the task or technology with the SME. The SME, knowing the job and the organization, is in the best position to explain the importance of the task or technology. If you do not have the SME tell you what is important, you may find that, when you write the introduction, the content that you have gathered does not provide adequate information for you to explain the importance of the task or technology.

Consider why the task or technology is important to PEMEO. *Why is the task or technology important for the worker, the job, and the organization?* You may also ask what the consequences are for PEMEO if:
- the task is performed poorly or not completed
- the technology functions abnormally or fails

Using terms and phrases

- Pay special attention to the use of terms and phrases. Ask the SME if a term is *correct*, or if people on the site *say it that way*. Confirm the use of terms such as *request, tell, ask*, and *demand*. By getting the terminology and phrasing correct, you will be more efficient in writing the module and will be more precise in using language that matches the customer's context.

- Sometimes a customer will use a slang term in lieu of the accepted industrial or scientific term. As an example, a

PART B Section 6
Conducting the Interview

customer may refer to a valve as *Old Blue* instead of valve V-104. Try to get the SME to agree to use the accepted term because others who come to the site may be using formal documentation such as Piping and Instrument Drawings to identify equipment. As a compromise you could put the slang term in brackets.

- Always get the definitions for acronyms.

Ask the SME specific questions relating to the performance statement or topic. Record his or her response on the computer. After several responses have been recorded, repeat back to the SME what you have written and get his or her approval or help the SME refine his or her explanations.

While you gather the content, question yourself as to the accuracy of the statements and continually search for missing information. If you think that a question you ask yourself is relevant, ask the SME. Apply the thinking strategies described in Part A for identifying relevant content.

With practice, you will develop your own mental strategy for applying relevant content criteria to identify content for modules. Here are two examples of strategies for applying LO–PEMEO relevant content criteria.

1. Use general categories of LO–PEMEO and work from the general to the specific. Mentally you can quickly eliminate many of the categories (e.g., impact on the safety of the operator) as being not applicable to a situation. When a category seems applicable, you can either ask about the impact relating to that category or be more precise as to the specific impact. For example: *What is the hazard? consequence?, control? regarding...*

2. Memorize the criteria (e.g., for safety) and do a mental search to determine if each criterion is applicable. Refer to Part A for questions regarding employee, job, and corporate performance.

As you continue interviewing and asking questions, from time to time refer to the sheet listing the corporate objectives as a guide to ensure relevant content has been identified. Use the list of corporate objectives to resolve any disagreement between you and the SME about whether or not specific content should be included in the training module.

In some cases, the SME doesn't want to include specific information in the module, whereas you want the information included to facilitate learning. To resolve this issue, refer to the criteria for relevant content (must have a task application or help make decisions and also contribute to the corporate objectives). Using the criteria is an objective means for determining if content is relevant and helps depersonalize the discussion and reduce the potential of conflict between you and the SME. If the content fits the criteria, then there is a good possibility that the content should be included. As an option, ask, *Does the trainee need to know this to do the work safely and effectively?*

If the answer is *Yes*, you may have to question the SME as to how the trainee acquired the knowledge or developed the skills. You may have to examine the assumptions made about prerequisite training and job experiences of the trainee.

Consider suggesting to the SME that experienced workers often forget the difficulties one can experience when learning, and may not appreciate that trainees require specific details to make learning effective and efficient.

Sometimes an SME may be quite adamant that specific content be included in the module but you don't think it should be. To determine the importance of the content, use these strategies:

1. Test the SME's conviction by asking him or her if it is important to write a test question for that topic.

2. Sometimes the content should be part of the training program but does not belong in the module for which you are gathering content. Identify the module that the content belongs in and make sure you immediately make a note of the fact in the scope document. Immediately documenting the information serves two purposes:
   - the SME is put at ease by being assured that the content will not be missed

- you are providing specific direction for developing the referenced module (another person might gather the content for the other module)

 Sometimes you and the SME may disagree about whether or not the content should be included in the module because the SME may not be considering instructional requirements. For example, the instruction must take into account the prerequisite training, job experiences, and learning abilities of the trainee. Detailed information should contribute to the learning process, but usually should **not** repeat training that the employee has already acquired (e.g., basic math concepts).

While interviewing, you can sometimes get over-involved in the technology and forget that the goal is to improve the trainee's performance and decision-making abilities. As a result, you may gather content that has only marginal payback for the customer.

Always question whether the content will contribute to improving the trainee's and the organization's performance. At the same time you must continue to search for missing information that will contribute to the trainee's effectiveness at doing the job and making decisions. As part of the interviewing process, using effective questioning techniques contributes to your ability to gather content that is valuable and complete.

Questioning techniques

Asking facilitative questions encourages the SME to continue to supply quality information. Give the SME enough time to think through the question. Ask only one question at a time. Use the following guidelines for asking facilitative questions:

- **Questions should relate to the competency** to keep the SME focused on the work at hand.

- **Use open-ended questions** when you need a general response. For example, *How do you start up the in-feed system? Why must the out-feed system be started before starting up the ball mill?*

- **Use closed questions** if you want specific responses. For example, *What is the voltage of the feed line to the motor for P-02? Is P-02 a centrifugal or positive displacement pump?*

- **Use precise terminology** when asking questions. For example, *in-feed* auger (not auger *thing*).

- **Do not use leading questions.** Leading questions imply a desired answer by using words such as *wouldn't* and *shouldn't*. For example, *Shouldn't the in-feed auger be started first?* Instead, ask, *What would happen if the in-feed auger was started first?*

- **Do not use loaded language.** Loaded questions imply a specific state of affairs. For example, *Is the company still taking safety shortcuts?* This question implies that the company took shortcuts in the past and is possibly still doing so, even if it is not true. Both yes and no would confirm that the company used to take safety shortcuts.

- **Don't ask questions that the SME likely will not be able to answer.** Instead of asking, *What are the design specifications for the in-feed auger?* you could ask, *Where can I get the design specifications for the in-feed auger?*

Throughout the interview, you will mostly be asking questions and telling the SME what you have recorded. Sometimes new consultants want to be recognized for their knowledge and tell the SME the specific information (content) that should be recorded. Generally, you should not provide content; the content may not reflect the organization and telling does not necessarily contribute to your credibility (especially if you are wrong).

If you have difficulty understanding the SME's explanations, you may find it beneficial to go on site with the SME and look at the equipment or observe the task being performed.

Alternatives to writing content

When gathering content, you may find that using words to describe the features and locations of components and equipment can be tedious to write and read. Consider

the following alternatives when gathering this type of information:
- labeled graphics
- plot plans
- component or equipment checklists (the trainee must go on site and locate and describe the function of each component or piece of equipment)

Taking photographs

Photographs of equipment may be helpful when writing the module. At some sites, you may need a Hot Work Permit and a combustible gas test because your camera may be a source of ignition (spark hazard). If you are taking photographs of several pieces of similar equipment, you may want to use a shot sheet (see Attachment 5—*Shot Sheet*) to identify the equipment in each shot. If you do not use a shot sheet, you may want to print the photographs and have the SME help label them.

Keeping the SME motivated

As the interview progresses, the SME may show signs of fatigue by wandering off topic, complaining about sitting for too long, saying that this type of work is very tiring, or showing irritation when answering questions. To make the best use of the contact time with the SME, pace the interview using the following techniques:
- take short breaks
- set small goals to be achieved before taking a break
- encourage the SME by discussing the progress made towards achieving the goal
- if he or she is off topic, repeat the last computer entry and ask what is next
- use humor
- carry out less mentally demanding activities such as sketching drawings, locating manuals and reference resources, taking photographs, or taking a site tour

At the end of the day, discuss the day's achievements and give the SME a word of encouragement for the progress that has been made. Plan the work for the next day to give the SME time to think about the topics.

Interviewing to Gather Relevant Content for Training

IMPORTANT Make at least one backup of the data files and store the backup in a location apart from your computer!

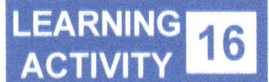

Gather the content

Gathering relevant content is achieved through the collaborative efforts of the SME and you. Throughout the interview, you need to provide leadership to ensure the content is relevant, useful, practical, and accurate.

The following questions apply to normal conditions unless otherwise stated. From the given choices, select the best answer to each question. Although other choices may apply under different conditions, do not consider these choices as being the best answers.

1. The benefit(s) of getting the SME to help identify the content for the introduction to a module is/are _____.

    a. critical information required for the introduction is identified
    b. wording can be selected that fits the customer's context
    c. you and the SME develop a better understanding of the purpose and importance of the training
    d. less time and effort are required to write the introduction to the module
    e. all of the above
    f. a and d only

2. What technique(s) can you use to identify relevant content?

    a. refer to the Topic Outline
    b. refer to the criteria for relevant content (tasks, decisions, corporate objectives).
    c. apply LO–PEMEO
    d. identify variables relating to the technology or process that the worker must monitor and control
    e. all of the above

PART B Section 6
Conducting the Interview

3. To identify relevant content, you should examine the training from the point of view of the _____.

   a. Trainee
   b. Coach
   c. Supervisor
   d. Consultant
   e. all of the above
   f. a and b only

4. When examining the gathered content to determine implications, you should try to identify the _____.

   a. cause
   b. effect
   c. consequence
   d. employee response if the expected action does not occur or a condition is abnormal
   e. all of the above

5. When using the 2-column content-gathering style sheet to record content on the computer, the left column describes the conditions of performance, the target audience, and the_____.

   a. observable behavior required to meet the standard of performance
   b. method of evaluating a trainee's performance
   c. required performance
   d. all of the above

6. When gathering content, you should pay special attention to _____.

   a. the use of terms and phrases
   b. the use of slang terminology
   c. definitions for acronyms
   d. all of the above

7. To determine whether specific content should be included in a module, you can _____.

   a. refer to the criteria for relevant content (task, decisions, corporate objectives)
   b. ask if the trainee needs to know this to do the work
   c. ask if a test question is necessary for the topic
   d. ask if the content belongs in another module
   e. any of the above

8. All content gathered during an interview should contribute to improving the trainee's and the organization's performance.

   a. true
   b. false

9. To obtain a specific response from an SME, you should ask _____ questions.

   a. open-ended
   b. leading
   c. closed
   d. loaded
   e. any of the above
   f. b and d only

10. While gathering content and recording the information on the computer, you should provide content wherever possible.

    a. true
    b. false

11. When gathering content describing components and equipment, in addition to using words, you could use _____.

    a. graphics
    b. plot plans
    c. component or equipment checklists
    d. all of the above
    e. a and b only

PART B Section 6
Conducting the Interview

12. Information provided in customer manuals is usually complete and adequately explained for training purposes.

    a. true

    b. false

13. To pace an interview with an SME, you can _____.

    a. take short breaks

    b. set small goals

    c. use humor

    d. carry out other activities

    e. all of the above

14. At the end of each day of content gathering, you should make a backup of the data files.

    a. true

    b. false

Answer Key

1.	e	6.	d	11.	d
2.	e	7.	e	12.	b
3.	e	8.	a	13.	e
4.	e	9.	c	14.	a
5.	c	10.	b		

Major Step 5—Refine the Content

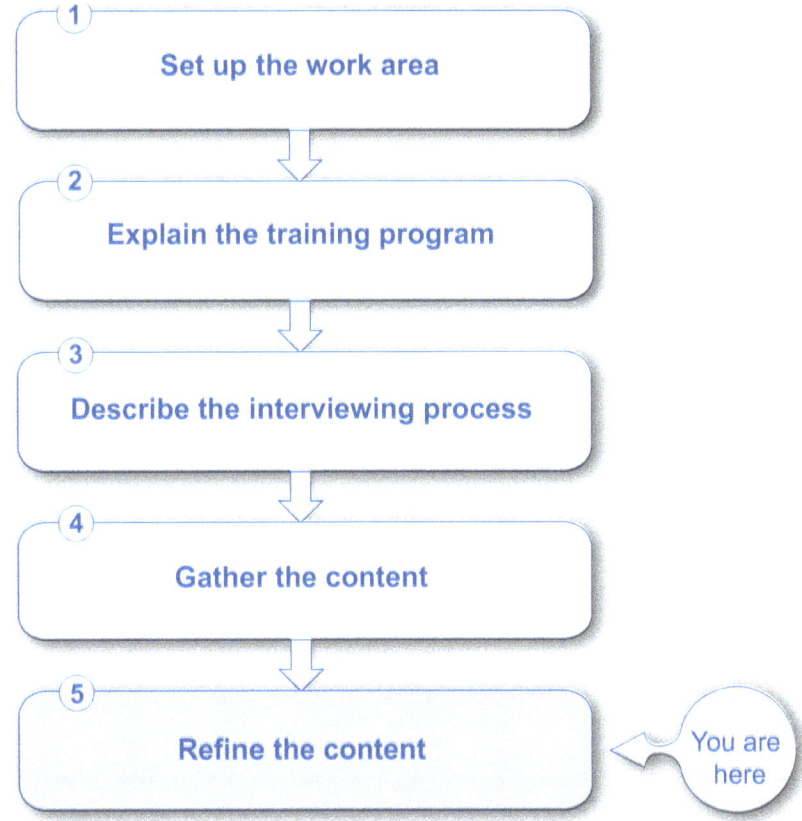

Gathering relevant content that is accurate and complete is essential for developing effective training resources. The quality of the content that you have gathered can be affected by several factors:

- the competence of the SME
- the ability of the SME to articulate the information in a logical order
- your ability to provide leadership by continually searching for missing content and questioning yourself about the accuracy of the information that the SME provided
- your ability to record content in words that reflect the SME's intended message
- the availability of reference resources

If the SME seems to know what he or she is talking about, you can be led into believing that the SME is

an unquestionable expert. You may then make several assumptions, including that the SME:
- knows exactly the type of information required for the training
- can identify (or remember) all the specifics about support knowledge and procedures required for the training
- always provides information that is accurate and correct

These assumptions may not always be correct, resulting in content that may be irrelevant, incomplete, or inaccurate. While you have access to the SME, review the content you have gathered to ensure it is accurate, complete, and understandable.

If you are interviewing the SME for two or more consecutive days, you should review the gathered content in the evening for quality. Often information that was recorded during the interview made sense at the time but, upon review, you discover ambiguities or missing information. Make sure you understand the content well enough to write instruction from which others can effectively learn. Does the support knowledge make sense to you? Do the procedures seem workable and include safety precautions? Make notes as to the content that needs clarification. Questions that the SME can probably answer can be discussed at the beginning of the next interview session. When reviewing gathered content, you should:
- Reorganize the content (if required) so that there is continuity of content and the order is suitable for writing the draft document. You will save time when planning the writing.
- Make sure you understand the support knowledge and that the procedures appear workable.
- Look for inaccuracies, ambiguities, and missing information.
- Tighten up the wording.
- Clean up the formats (especially first and second indents and sub-information for procedures).
- Spell check the document.
- Print the file, if practical, to review with the SME.

Ideally, when you have completed gathering the content, you will have a document that is a point-form version of the final training module. Graphics, references, and ideas for presenting the information will be documented. Don't leave any information to memory. Information can be forgotten because of the complexity of the work and delays in writing the module. Keep in mind that someone else may have to write the module from the content and directions that you provide.

If the gathered content is relatively complete, you may want to give a paper copy to the SME for review. Depending on the arrangements made with the customer, the gathered content may also need to be validated by other customer personnel. If the content is going to be circulated among other customer personnel, clean up the formats before printing the draft.

Normally, customers validate the draft products to ensure they are correct, complete, and what they want. Often the validation process is discussed and arranged as part of planning the content gathering and resource development process. See Section 5—*Planning Interviewing Sessions*.

Section 7

Using SMEs Who are not Part of the Group Receiving Training

Sometimes you may find it necessary to get specific information from personnel who work in other departments and who are not part of the target audience (e.g., getting information from accountants, electricians, millwrights, or engineers for a training program designed for operators). Sometimes the external SME may be a representative from a vendor, manufacturer, or government agency. Using an external SME can pose special problems:

- The external SME may not understand what the target audience needs to know to do its job safely and effectively. In this situation, the external SME may provide the wrong information or information that is too detailed. To get the required information, provide the external SME with the following information:
  - a brief explanation of the training program (i.e., developing a training program for...). You do not have to explain the program in detail.
  - the type of information required

Interviewing to Gather Relevant Content for Training

- how the target audience will use the information
- the reason you contacted him or her for information

- The external SME may want to change the duties of the target audience. This situation may arise when two departments work closely together and their work affects each other. For example, maintenance staff may want operators to do more, to leave things alone, or to do things differently. Usually it is not your mandate to change job descriptions or job functions of the target audience. Tell the external SME that it is not your mandate to change work arrangements and that, if changes are desired, normal communication channels should be used to initiate the changes.

After gathering content from the external SME, get an experienced customer SME to review the content to ensure the information meets both work and training requirements.

Section 8
The Consultant's Role

Previous sections of this book addressed (directly or indirectly) some roles of a training consultant or technical writer. This section provides a cohesive description of these roles.

As a training consultant or technical writer, you have a difficult role to play because of potentially conflicting expectations. On the one hand, you are expected to provide leadership and direction. On the other hand, you are expected to work with customer's management and operational strategies, but not to tell the organization how to do its business.

The customer has specific expectations and beliefs about your qualifications and your role as a consultant:
- You have specialized skills and abilities that the customer's personnel do not have.
- As a representative of your organization, you will perform specific services and your efforts will contribute to the customer's objectives.
- You will provide leadership and direction in developing useful and practical performance and training resources.
- You will be facilitative in dealing with the customer's personnel and will not impose your personal beliefs or biases.

- If there is a concern about training program design, you will point out the cons and pros to the customer and may make recommendations with the understanding that the customer makes the final decision.

During the course of the interview session, the SME may bring up political or controversial issues relating to the company or to the job. It is best for you to remain neutral and non-committal, perhaps by rephrasing any comments without being judgmental or taking a position (e.g., *So you're saying that...*).

You should make the effort to develop excellent working relationships with customers. Sometimes you may develop a strong personal relationship with the SME and may spend time together off the job. As a result of this relationship, you can develop an allegiance with the SME that could be detrimental to your consulting role, for example:
- You could buy into the SME's beliefs or position regarding the organization (e.g., union versus management).
- You could divulge confidential information about the customer and your organization or department that could have negative implications.

To maintain your effectiveness as a training consultant or technical writer, remind yourself that you represent your organization and that your mandate is to meet the customer's expectations. Indirectly (or possibly directly), you are being paid by the customer to perform specific services and to contribute to the customer's objectives.

Sometimes you may have difficulty getting the customer's cooperation. The customer may not provide SMEs when they are needed or may provide an SME who is not able to provide quality content. Generally, when these situations arise, you should let your supervisor or the person you report to resolve the issues. By minimizing your involvement, you will be able to maintain a good working relationship with the SMEs. Your supervisor should take the initiative to resolve the issues in a way that maintains a positive customer relationship. For example, if an SME is not doing a good job, your supervisor should work with the customer to find a means of replacing that person in a way that doesn't offend him or her.

Customers expect you to provide direction and take initiative to efficiently produce quality products. To maintain your reputation (or your organization's), it is important that the customer perceive you as a leader. If the SME is exceptionally good, you may not have to provide a great deal of leadership. The SME knows what is important for training (relevant content) and can organize and present the information effectively. You end up doing more typing and less questioning to gather relevant content. In this situation you could be perceived as a scribe or expensive secretary. To be perceived as providing leadership during the interview, ask a lot of questions and feed the responses back to the SME. Question the use of terms and phrases. Try to tighten up wording. Set goals and develop a work plan for yourself and the SME.

During the interviews, you may identify issues that could have a negative impact on your organization or the customer. For example:
- The work is more complex than expected and will take longer to complete than planned. The result will be a budget over-run.
- More time than anticipated will be needed with the SME.
- There is talk that the customer wants to develop training internally.
- You are gathering content for a competency and the customer is considering modifying some of the technology. Any training resources that you develop based on the present technology will have to be rewritten.
- The SME does not want to include specific safety precautions because he or she thinks that the company's policy is to save money or take short cuts.
- Employees use unsafe practices because the technology doesn't work properly.
- Environmental laws are being broken.

If you identify any of these issues, discuss the issues with your supervisor or the person to whom you report to determine what action, if any, should be taken. Your supervisor needs your input and support because issues are often unique or have a special *twist* to them from previous issues. You and your supervisor must work cooperatively to decide on the best course of action.

In addition to providing quality services and products, many other factors contribute to a customer's **perception** of your organization's reputation. Although you may not understand all the implications for the customer or for your organization, it is important that you follow through in a timely and effective manner on your supervisor's directions to respond to customer concerns. By taking appropriate action, you are demonstrating that you have your customer's best interests in mind. Serving the customer well and showing interest in the customer's wellbeing contributes to the development of long-term relationships with that customer. Customers who are satisfied with your services and products are the best promoters of your services.

If you do not follow through on your supervisor's directions or do not carry out the course of action that you and your supervisor have agreed to, there is a possibility that your own and/or your organization's credibility may be damaged. Contracts could be cut back or new contracts awarded to competitors.

Section 9

Summary

The interviewing procedures described in this book are based on HDC's twenty-five plus years of practical experience conducting interviews to gather and organize relevant training content. The most important concern for customers is that the content of training or reference resources addresses their business issues. Part A identifies thinking strategies you can use to identify relevant content that will have excellent value for your customers.

As a training consultant or technical writer, you need to promote the value of the products or program you are developing. The long-term goal is for the user group to recognize the value of the resources in contributing to improved employee, job, and corporate performance.

Many of the pitfalls that can occur during an interview and possible solutions have been addressed. Knowing the pitfalls can help you be better prepared to deal with them.

Part B addresses the interviewing process. HDC has found that consultants who follow the recommended interviewing process have excellent success in gathering relevant content. Generally, consultants run into difficulty when they stray from the recommended interviewing process without understanding the implications of making the changes. Attachment 3— *Interviewing Checklist* summarizes the interviewing steps explained in this book. You may use a different content-gathering format than the one described in the checklist; however, the overall interview process works well.

When interviewing, use the thinking strategies and relevant content questions identified in Attachment 6—*Relevant Content Questions*. You can also use this list for determining types of information that could be considered for a competency.

You may find interviewing the customer's SMEs to be one of the more challenging and enjoyable aspects of your job. The interview is a cooperative process in which you and the SME each use your individual expertise to identify relevant content for training.

To meet the customer's expectations, it is essential that during the interview you gather content that is accurate, complete, and relevant to the tasks that the customer's employees perform. Gathering quality content leads to the efficient development of quality training resources, requiring little rework or additional research.

Always keep in mind that the key purpose of interviewing the SME is to identify and structure relevant content so that:
- the training will improve people's performance
- the information will help you write training resources and test instruments

The interviewing techniques and processes described in this book are based on an ideal content-gathering scenario. You may find that you have to use other methods to gather content including conducting telephone interviews and doing literature searches. Regardless of the method used to gather the content, the key criteria used to select relevant content remain the same:
- task application
- decision-making
- the audience's qualifications
- the prerequisite and co-requisite training
- corporate objectives
- safety and loss control
- desired training outcomes

PART B Section 9
Summary

Always keep the key criteria for relevant content in mind when planning development, gathering content, and developing training resources and test instruments.

Refining the content, using external SMEs, and consultant roles

Throughout the interview, you must ensure the gathered content is relevant, useful, practical, accurate, and complete. You must effectively carry out your role as a consultant or technical writer to ensure customer satisfaction and to maintain long-term relations with the customer.

The following questions apply to normal conditions unless otherwise stated. From the given choices, select the best answer to each question. Although other choices may apply under different conditions, do not consider these choices as being the best answers.

1. To refine gathered content, you should _____.
   a. reorganize the content if necessary
   b. tighten up wording and clean up formats
   c. spell check
   d. all of the above

2. Arrangements for validating content gathered during an interview should be made before going to the site.
   a. true
   b. false

3. Problems associated with gathering content from an *external SME* include _____.
   a. lack of understanding of the target audience
   b. attempting to change the duties of the target audience
   c. providing information that is inappropriate or too detailed
   d. all of the above

  e. a and b only

  f. b and c only

4. After content is gathered from an *external SME*, the content should be reviewed by _____.

  a. your supervisor

  b. a different external SME

  c. an experienced customer SME

  d. all of the above

5. Customers expect you to _____.

  a. have specialized skills and abilities that their staff do not have

  b. contribute to their corporate objectives

  c. provide leadership and direction to develop training resources

  d. all of the above

6. If the SME raises political or controversial issues, it is best for you to _____.

  a. sympathize with the SME

  b. remain neutral and non-committal

  c. defend the customer's corporate objectives

  d. report the incident to your supervisor

7. If you work for a consulting firm and have difficulty getting the customer's cooperation, you alone are responsible for resolving the issue.

  a. true

  b. false

8. To reinforce the perception of providing leadership during an interview, you should _____.

  a. ask a lot of questions and feed the responses back to the SME

b. question the use of terms and phrases and tighten up wording

c. set goals and develop a work plan

d. all of the above

9. If you identify an issue which could have a negative impact on your organization, your first response should be to _____.

   a. debate the issue with the SME
   b. inform the customer's management of the issue
   c. discuss the issue with your supervisor
   d. make a record of the issue and wait for new developments before taking further action
   e. any of the above

Answer Key

1. d
2. a
3. d
4. c
5. d
6. b
7. b
8. d
9. c

Section 10

Suggested Exercises

The best way to learn and refine interviewing skills is to practice. The following exercises have been segmented so that practice times are manageable. If the exercises are to be used by a consulting firm, the exercises and attachments may have to be modified to be a better match with existing interviewing processes.

Exercise 1: Acquire the support knowledge

Read this book and answer the Learning Activity questions. You should be able to answer all the questions correctly before going on to Exercise 2.

Exercise 2: Practice interviewing

The following practice sessions are based on the assumption that you are employed by a consulting firm. If you are freelancing, you can practice doing parts of this exercise when interviewing SMEs. The practice will hone your skills and help determine which interviewing strategies work best for you.

To complete Exercise 2, several practice interview sessions should be scheduled with each session covering a specific

Interviewing to Gather Relevant Content for Training

part of the interviewing process. Before each session, review the applicable part of Attachment 3—*Interviewing Checklist*. During each session, your coach will give you a demonstration and you will then demonstrate the skills back to your coach. The following training sequence has been divided into sessions. The order of the sessions can be changed as circumstances dictate. Each session can be repeated if you need more practice.

Session 1
- Coach demonstrates **Major Step 1**—*Set up the work area*.
- Coach demonstrates **Major Step 2**—*Explain the training program*.
- You demonstrate **Major Step 2**—*Explain the training program*.

Session 2
- You set up the work area.
- Coach demonstrates **Major Step 3**—*Describe Interviewing Process*.
- You demonstrate **Major Step 3**—*Describe Interviewing Process*.
- Coach demonstrates **Major Step 4**—*Gather the Content* using a third person as the SME.
- Coach demonstrates **Major Step 4**—*Gather the Content* using you as the SME.

Session 3
- You demonstrate **Major Step 4**—*Gather the Content* using a third person as SME. The Coach observes the interview and gives you feedback after the interview is completed.
- You complete **Major Step 5**—*Refine the Content* and submit a copy to the Coach and SME.
- Coach and SME review your work and give you feedback.

Session 4
- You set up the work area.
- You demonstrate **Major Step 4**—*Gather the Content* using a third person as SME.
- You complete **Major Step 5**—*Refine the Content* and submit a copy to the SME.
- SME reviews the work and gives you feedback.

PART B Section 10
Suggested Exercises

- You write up part of the module including the following items:
  - training objectives
  - introduction
  - part of body of module
  - multiple-choice questions and/or checklist
- Coach reviews written work and gives you feedback.

Options
- Observe an experienced consultant conduct an interview with a customer's SME.
- Write a module using an experienced consultant's gathered content.
- Have the coach observe you interview a new SME:
  - complete **Major Steps 1, 3, 4,** and **5**. The coach could do **Major Step 2**.
  - note that the coach will probably not observe the entire interview
  - refine the gathered content and submit it to the coach
  - the coach reviews the content you have gathered
  - the coach gives you feedback about your interview and the gathered content

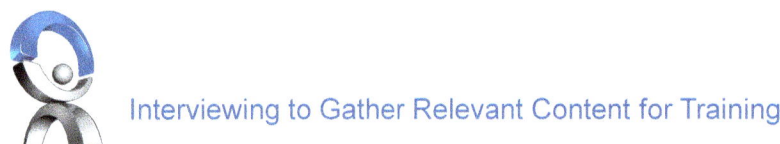

■ Attachments

Attachment 1 — A1-1
Purpose and Benefits of Interviewing the Customer's Experienced Staff

Attachment 2 — A2-1
Project and Interview Preparation Checklists

Attachment 3 — A3-1
Interviewing Checklist

Attachment 4 — A4-1
Examples of Module Outlines for Content Gathering (sometimes called Expanded Scope)

Attachment 5 — A5-1
Shot Sheet

Attachment 6 — A6-1
Relevant Content Questions

ATTACHMENT 1

Purpose and Benefits of Interviewing the Customer's Experienced Staff

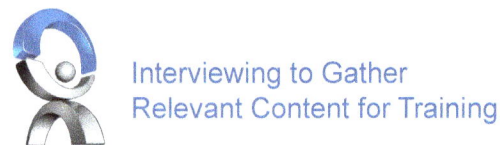

Interviewing to Gather Relevant Content for Training

**Attachment 1
Purpose and Benefits of Interviewing the Customer's Experienced Staff**

1. The objectives and gathered content establish the customer's expectations as to what should be put into their training program and to what degree of detail.

2. The objectives and gathered content define the knowledge and skills that are observable, repeatable, and measurable (i.e., there is a means of establishing and measuring competence).

3. The objectives and gathered content specify the criteria used to evaluate the trainee and suggest how to carry out the evaluation.

4. The objectives and gathered content separate critical knowledge and skills from information that either is nice to know or assists learning so that the training is effective and efficient. In addition, training resource development time and costs are minimized.

5. The objectives and gathered content provide the consultant with the opportunity to determine the best methods of delivering the training for the specific target group in their specific environment:
   - self study, checklists
   - demonstrations, lecture, tapes, etc.
   - reading level
   - appropriate analogies, diagrams, charts, etc.
   - other learning activities both on and off the job

6. The interviewing process provides a means of collecting data for developing the training resources.

7. The interviewing and validation process ensures the information is accurate and complete which directly benefits the customer, the consultant, and HDC (job-focused, cost-effective, safe, legal, customer satisfaction).

8. The content-gathering process provides a means for the consultant and the SME to examine the gathered content without claiming the information will be part of the training program. As a result, changes can be made objectively, without resistance, and without damaging the SME's esteem.

9. Determining that the trainee will be assessed about specific content confirms the content has value for training.

10. The process of gathering and validating both the objectives and the content contributes to the customer's knowledge of the training program design, training delivery strategies, and training evaluation methods.

11. The process of gathering and validating the objectives and the content establishes the customer's ownership of the training program. Having the customer's employees give input encourages them to accept the program as being beneficial for themselves and the company.

12. Documenting objectives and content provides a mechanism for organizing the program in ways that facilitate training and provide the least disruption to the day-to-day requirements of the job (e.g., general to specific, sequentially, developmentally, integrationally, flexibly). Further, these instructional design opportunities occur throughout the process.

ATTACHMENT 2

Project and Interview Preparation Checklists

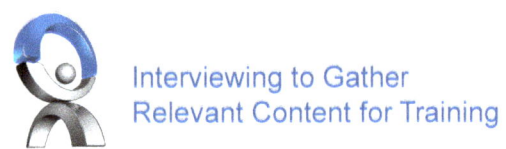

Interviewing to Gather
Relevant Content for Training

Attachment 2
Project and Interview
Preparation Checklists

Part 1 – Project Preparation Checklist

The project leader provides the following information to the consultant:

- ☐ customer's training goals
- ☐ customer's training program scope
- ☐ client's corporate objectives
- ☐ the type of technology or processes used by the customer
- ☐ the target audience and its qualifications:
  - formal education
  - experience level
  - prerequisite training
  - tasks performed by the audience
- ☐ the work assignment
- ☐ the relationship of the training that the consultant will develop with the rest of the customer's training program
- ☐ module design requirements
- ☐ the validation process
- ☐ specific content resources to take to the site
- ☐ the type of technical knowledge the consultant requires before starting work
- ☐ the SME's qualifications:
  - job position and work experiences
  - knowledge of and involvement in the training program
- ☐ the meeting arrangements:
  - date and time of the meeting
  - travel arrangements
  - accommodations
  - the SME's name and phone number
  - other pertinent customer personnel that can contribute to the program development process or can influence the project (including sensitivities of specific personnel)
  - directions to the site
  - ☐ lunch arrangements
  - ☐ the appropriate dress code including safety requirements

Part 2 – Interview Preparation Checklist

The consultant prepares the following types of resources for the interview:

Computer Supplies

- ☐ computer
- ☐ computer cables (power, keyboard, internet)
- ☐ keyboard
- ☐ mouse and mouse pad
- ☐ backup hardware (UPS memory stick)
- ☐ extension cord and power bar
- ☐ if necessary, printer, printer cable, power cable, printer paper, additional ink cartridge

Stationery and Photographic Supplies

- ☐ pads of paper (including graph paper for drawing diagrams)
- ☐ pens
- ☐ pencils
- ☐ highlighters
- ☐ colored markers
- ☐ *Post-it* Notes
- ☐ camera and accessories (if photographs are necessary)
- ☐ extra batteries for camera
- ☐ Shot Sheet (if necessary)

 Interviewing to Gather Relevant Content for Training

Support Documents

- ☐ training profile
- ☐ scope document
- ☐ module outlines (if available)
- ☐ samples of training modules
- ☐ samples of content gathered from similar interview sessions
- ☐ relevant content criteria

Part 3 – SME Preparation Checklist

The Consultant

- ☐ discusses the following issues with the SME:
  - meeting date, time, and location
  - work assignment
  - working relationship
- ☐ e-mails the scope document or module outline to the SME
- ☐ couriers similar modules to the SME (if available)
- ☐ instructs the SME to bring documents to the meeting such as:
  - operations manuals
  - safety manuals
  - vendor manuals
  - process drawings
  - written procedures
  - quality standards (e.g., ISO 9000)

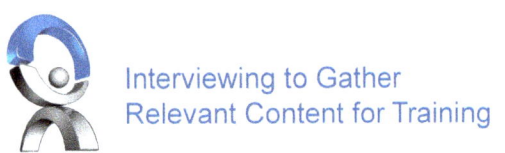

Interviewing to Gather Relevant Content for Training

ATTACHMENT 3

Interviewing Checklist

Interviewing to Gather
Relevant Content for Training

Attachment 3
Interviewing Checklist

Part 1 – Set Up The Work Area

- [ ] Select a work location that:
  - is close to the SME's work
  - is quiet
  - has adequate lighting and heating
  - is free from distractions

- [ ] Arrange the work area by:
  - positioning the SME either at right angles or across from you
  - clearing space for writing and viewing documents

  Note: If setting up in someone's office, minimize disturbance of the occupant's work.

- [ ] Set up the computer.

- [ ] Discuss safety requirements for entering the work area.

- [ ] If drinking coffee, ask about the coffee fund.

- [ ] Consider asking if the SME smokes (affects pacing).

Part 2 – Explain The Training Program

- [ ] Ask the SME about his or her knowledge of the training program.

- [ ] From the following lists, explain the parts of the training program that the SME does **not** know about.

Purpose and importance of training program (customer-specific)

- [ ] The training program has many benefits for your company and employees such as:

  (From the following list, select those benefits that best suit the customer. You can also add benefits that are applicable to the customer.)
  - providing a structured method for delivering training
  - ensuring efficient and effective training
  - improving safety
  - minimizing losses
  - ensuring employees do NOT do tasks they have not been trained to do
  - ensuring employees are all trained to the same level of competence so that they can do the job the way you and your company want the job done
  - reducing stress (employees, team leader, supervisor, etc.)
  - recognizing employees for their abilities
  - requiring you and other employees to help develop the training so the training fits your company and the way it does business

Profile

- [ ] Is a visual way of presenting information (a list could be used).

- [ ] Was developed by a small group of your staff and then validated by other staff.

- [ ] Provides a framework and structure for the training program and helps plan the development of training resources.

- [ ] Identifies knowledge and skills (competencies) a person needs to do his or her job safely and effectively.

- [ ] Groups related competencies to form a band (give an example).

- [ ] Codes bands and competencies for ease of identification.

- [ ] Starts each competency with a verb because the focus is on people and their performance.

  Note: Titles for existing courses provided by outside agencies or by the customer may not start with verbs.

- [ ] Provides an observable way for people to show that they have acquired the knowledge and skills (i.e., demonstrates competence).

Interviewing to Gather Relevant Content for Training

Attachment 3
Interviewing Checklist

Scope

- ☐ A scope is prepared for each competency to explain the critical knowledge and skills that the training will address. Otherwise, it may be difficult to tell what the competency statements mean or cover.

- ☐ We can add to or change the scope as we get into detail when we develop the training for a competency.

Delivering and Administering Training

- ☐ Your organization will have control of the training and will plan and track the training.

- ☐ The specifics about administering the training program have not been worked out yet.

- ☐ A variety of methods may be used to deliver the training.
  - Some local agencies can deliver some of the training such as First Aid.
  - Perhaps some of your people already deliver government-required courses such as TDG and WHMIS.
  - Your people will deliver much of the training using self-instructional modules and on-the-job coaching.

- ☐ Your training program will overcome many of the weaknesses of buddy-system training such as:
  - passing on bad habits
  - forgetting to tell and show the trainee all the critical things about the job
  - having no formal way of knowing if the trainee has acquired the knowledge and can do the work the way you would want it done

Self-Instructional Module

- ☐ **Title** closely matches the wording of the competency listed on the Training Profile.

- ☐ **Training Objectives**
  - Specify what employees must know and be able to do.
  - If employees know what is expected of them, they tend to work towards achieving those expectations.

- ☐ **Introduction**
  - Provides an overview of the module content.
  - Explains the purpose and importance of the technology and tasks addressed in the module.
  - Provides the *big picture* by explaining the relationship of the technology addressed in the module to related technology and how the tasks fit into the job and impact other people.
  - Prepares the trainee for learning.

- ☐ **Text**
  - The content is customized to meet your organization's unique requirements and expectations.
  - The content is selected to ensure the training is practical and beneficial to your organization and its employees.
  - The content is presented in a way that is highly structured and developmental to lead the trainee to achieve the learning objectives.
  - The content will be specific, accurate, and comprehensive to provide good instruction and be useful to the trainee in learning his or her job.

- ☐ **Review Questions**
  - Address the critical knowledge associated with the training objectives.
  - Provide the answers to the questions so that the trainee can check his or her learning.

- ☐ **Knowledge Check**
  - Is used to *confirm* that the trainee has acquired the knowledge presented in the module.
  - Is made by rewording and reordering the review questions.

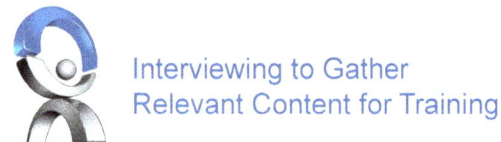

Interviewing to Gather Relevant Content for Training

Attachment 3
Interviewing Checklist

- If the trainee can correctly answer all the review questions, then he or she should be able to correctly answer all the knowledge check questions. If a question is answered incorrectly, the person doing the checking can ask the question orally to ensure the trainee didn't misunderstand the question.

☐ **Performance Check (Checklist)**
- Specifies the step-by-step actions required to carry out a task.
- In some cases, there is more than one way of doing a task but, for training purposes, only one method should be used.

☐ **Mastery Learning**
- For safety and productivity reasons, it is important that the trainee can answer all the questions correctly and carry out the tasks according to your organization's expectations.
- The training is efficient and effective because the expectations are clearly stated at the beginning of training and then everything is done to help the trainee learn quickly and effectively.
- For coaching to be effective, there must be no secrets or surprises; certainly this is different from traditional education.
- We have found for other customers that once their employees start using the training program, they really like the mastery training approach.

Part 3 – Describe The Interviewing Process

If the SME has **not** provided content before, provide the following explanation of the interviewing process.

☐ The interviewing process is effective because it uses both your and my talents. You know your company and the job the best, and I have the educational and training background.

☐ I will ask lots of questions and type your explanations directly into the computer.

☐ Show an example of gathered content and explain the key features:

Header
- Module number and name, date, consultant's and SME's names
- SME's name is important so that I or another consultant will know who to contact if there are further questions

Body
- I will record the conditions and the target audience's performance. In the module, this information is used for developing training objectives and identifying titles for the sections.
- I will record the specific knowledge and actions expected of the target audience.
- I will use the point form information to develop the specific content of the training module. To develop the module, I will apply educational concepts, convert the point form information into sentences and paragraphs, and add graphics as required.

☐ After gathering the content in point form, I will clean up the format and grammar and will give you a chance to review the work if you wish.

☐ During the interview, some information may be missed because that's the nature of conducting interviews.

☐ Other workers at your company will look at the draft module to add their own ideas as to how things work and how to do the job and also to check for accuracy and completeness.

☐ If you wish, I could send the draft module to you first for your review.

☐ Identifying the required content and the amount of detail can be difficult. All kinds of training could be developed but it is important to limit the training so that the

A3-4

training is practical, directly benefits the company and employees, and is cost-effective.

☐ To ensure the right type of content is addressed in the training module, we use criteria for relevant content.

Note: You have several choices as to the amount of detail and the method used to present relevant content criteria:
• write the criteria
• use a prepared list or chart

☐ Show the SME the criteria and provide the following explanation:
• All of the training must culminate in a practical application—people performing tasks and making decisions.
• For training to be of most value to the organization, the training must contribute to and reinforce the **corporate objectives**.
• To perform tasks safely and effectively, employees must have **knowledge** of the technology and processes. Senior employees must understand why things work the way they do, the impact that employees can have on the technology, and cause and effect issues. For training to be cost-effective, the knowledge must have a practical application. An important question we always ask is, *Does the employee have to know this to do his or her job well?*
• Employees must also understand the **supervisor's expectations** and lines of authority.
• To be able to work with others and communicate effectively, employees must also understand the management and **administration system.**
• Last, but not least, for employees to make effective **decisions**, they must be able to consider job and company-related criteria including:
  – procedures for tasks
  – corporate objectives
  – technology
  – management and administration protocols
  – lines of authority
  – limits of authority
  – roles and responsibilities

☐ We will use the relevant content criteria in three different ways:
• to identify training content
• after we've gathered content, to check if all important content has been identified
• to help us decide if specific content should be included or left out. If the content fits the criteria, the content should probably be included. If the content does not fit the criteria, the content should probably be left out.

☐ Ask the SME if he or she agrees with the criteria for selecting relevant content.

☐ If the SME disagrees with relevant content criteria, discuss differences and work out an agreement.

Part 4 – Gather The Content

Major Step 1—*Select the first competency to work on*

☐ Identify the competencies for which content must be gathered.

☐ Identify the related competencies.

☐ Discuss the level of complexity and specific issues associated with each competency for which content must be gathered.

☐ Determine the personal preference for competency content-gathering sequence but do **not** indicate preference to the SME at this time. Your personal preferences could be based on:
• personal knowledge of content

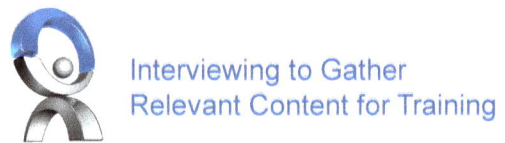

Interviewing to Gather Relevant Content for Training

Attachment 3
Interviewing Checklist

- personal learning style (e.g., general to specific)
- advantage of developing procedures for tasks before identifying content for knowledge-focused modules

☐ Ask the SME which competency he or she would like to work on first.

Note: Some of the issues that could affect the SME's decision include:
- level of expertise in content areas
- personal likes or dislikes for specific technology, processes, or tasks
- wanting to start with an easy competency to learn about the expectations for providing content
- availability of specific documentation relating to module content

☐ If necessary, negotiate with the SME to determine which competency to work on first.

Major Step 2—*Identify the audience and training sequence*

☐ Identify the audience:
- formal education
- specialized external training
- experience in the present position
- previously completed competencies

☐ Identify the training outcomes (tasks, knowledge, or both).

☐ Identify the relationship of competency to prerequisite and advanced competencies.

☐ Identify the related competencies.

☐ Determine the requirements for the competency in relation to work flow and production requirements (work assignments based on production requirements and staffing changes).

Major Step 3—*Identify the job applications*

☐ Identify the job applications of the training (tasks and decision making to which the training will contribute)

☐ If the competency addresses a task(s), identify critical issues associated with the task(s) and decision making such as:
- frequency that the task is performed
- preconditions that require the task to be performed
- conditions under which the task must be performed
- difficulty of performing the task
- critical issues when performing the task that affect people, equipment, materials, environment, and organization (PEMEO)
- standard for performing the task (e.g., indicators, ISO 9000, performance statements, specifications embedded in procedures)
- possible consequences if the task is not performed satisfactorily

Major Step 4—*Develop the topical outline*

☐ If the module outline was prepared in advance, get the SME's *approval* of the outline, including:
- outcome
- audience
- topics
- prerequisite assumptions
- methods of assessment

☐ If the module outline was not prepared in advance:
- Say to the SME, *Before we begin, tell me about (technology, process, or task)*.
- Casually lean back in the chair and relax to put the SME at ease.
- Listen closely to identify the main topics and to determine the order in which the topics might be sequenced.

A3-6

Interviewing to Gather Relevant Content for Training

Attachment 3
Interviewing Checklist

- Take notes if necessary (e.g., if the SME's explanation is complex).
- If the SME is NOT providing quality information, provide additional prompts such as:
  - *What are the main components of the process?*
  - *What are the major steps for completing the task?*
- Suggest a topic outline, excluding the *Introduction* (write in point form or draw a flow diagram).
- Get the SME's *approval* of the topic outline including:
  - outcome
  - audience
  - topics
  - prerequisite assumptions
  - methods of assessment
- Suggest that an *Introduction* is also required.

Options

☐ Expand the topic outline into a module outline.

☐ Immediately validate the module outline.

Major Step 5—*Gather and record relevant content*

☐ Call up the Content-Gathering Style Sheet on the computer.

☐ Save the file using the module name/number.

☐ Open the *Header* and fill in data.

☐ Ask the SME for the spelling of his or her name or repeat the name as you type it.

☐ Close the *Header*.

☐ Record the following information:
  - conditions
  - target audience
  - etc.

☐ Ask questions about the specific performance.

☐ Type in the SME's responses.

☐ After several entries, read back the information you entered in the computer.

☐ Ensure the terms and phrases are used correctly.

☐ Mentally search for missing information to ensure the key types of content have been considered for putting into the module:
  - Refer to the topic outline.
  - Refer to the *Criteria for Relevant Content*.
  - Apply LO-PEMEO.
  - Examine training and performance situations from the trainee's, coach's, supervisor's, and consultant's points of view and needs.
  - Consider reasons, causes, effects, consequences, and what if it doesn't work.
  - Identify variables and consequences if variables change.

☐ If in doubt about the value of content that the SME provides, ask, *Does the trainee need to know this to do his or her job?* If the answer is yes, ask, *Does the trainee have the prerequisite training, knowledge, or experience?*

Warning: Save and back up the computer file regularly.

☐ Use pacing techniques to keep the SME engaged in the work:
  - Set goals for the day.
  - Set goals to be completed before taking breaks.
  - Discuss progress towards achieving goals.
  - Take short breaks.
  - Change the work assignment (e.g., look for written data, draw diagrams).

A3-7

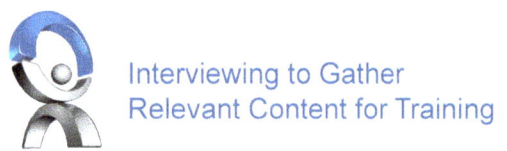

Interviewing to Gather Relevant Content for Training

Attachment 3
Interviewing Checklist

☐ To help write the module, get resources such as:
- graphics
- maps
- charts
- computer printouts
- plot plans
- flow diagrams
- P&IDs
- hand-drawn sketches
- equipment and operating specifications
- photographs

Note: Make sure the information on hand drawings is legible and written in full. Clearly label all hand drawings to avoid any future misinterpretations.

Note: Label resources that must be returned to the customer with:
- Company
- Location
- Person

☐ At the end of the day:
- Give the SME a word of encouragement for the progress that has been made.
- Plan the next day's work.

Warning: Make at least one backup of the data files. Do **not** store the backup file(s) with the computer.

Part 5 – Refine The Content

- Reorganize the content as required.
- Make sure you understand the support knowledge and that the procedures appear workable.
- Look for inaccuracies, ambiguities, and missing information.
- Tighten up the wording.
- Clean up the formats (especially the 1st and 2nd indents).
- Spell-check the document.
- Print a hard copy.
- Evaluate the content for ambiguities and missing information.
- Make notes of questions to ask the SME to clarify content.
- Give the SME a hard copy of the content for review if the content is relatively complete.

Note: If the content is to be validated by several customer staff, have your production staff clean up the formats and produce copies for distribution.

ATTACHMENT 4

Examples of Module Outlines for Content Gathering (sometimes called Expanded Scope)

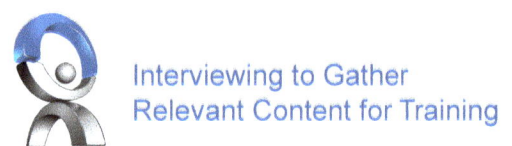

Interviewing to Gather Relevant Content for Training

Attachment 4
Examples of Module Outlines for Content Gathering (sometimes called Expanded Scope)

J12 – Describe Basics of Cathodic Protection

Target Audiences: First or second year apprentice electricians and operators

Key Tasks: Take readings, document, adjust, troubleshoot, isolate cathodic system to repair protected equipment

Content Scope

1. **Introduction**
   - definition of corrosion
   - definition of cathodic protection
   - purpose and importance of cathodic protection
   - benefits (implications for company and site)
   - key operating issue: need to operate system at specific parameters
   - general operator and maintenance personnel involvement
   - overview of critical safety considerations:
     – hazards when servicing/repairing protected equipment
     – loss control measures

2. **Principles of Operation**
   - general theory
     – concept of cathodic protection
     – current requirements
     – circuit resistance
   - sacrificial anode
     – main components
     – basic theory of operation
     – application
   - impressed current
     – main components
     – basic theory of operation
     – application
   - electrical sources
     – AC/DC rectifier
     – thermal electric generator
   - applications of cathodic protection systems including protection of aluminum fuel gas lines

3. **Monitor and Adjust Cathodic Protection System**
   - sacrificial anode
   - impressed current
     – AC/DC rectifier
     – thermal electric generator
     – taking readings
   - documentation
   - making adjustments
   - troubleshooting and decision making

4. **Maintain and Repair Cathodic Protection System**
   - common damage to anode beds and their repair
   - repairing rectifiers
   - isolating protected equipment requiring repair
     – tag and lockout
   - avoiding the protection of bare structures
   - maintaining cathodic protection insulation
   - regulatory requirements
     – standards and codes

Interviewing to Gather Relevant Content for Training

Attachment 4
Examples of Module Outlines for Content Gathering (sometimes called Expanded Scope)

J25 – Describe and Maintain Compressor Panels

Target Audiences: Instrumentation technicians and third year apprentice electricians

Key Tasks: Install new panels or replace existing panels (pneumatic and electronic), calibrate panels, troubleshoot panels, maintain documents

Content Scope

1. **Introduction**
   - purpose and importance of compressor panels
   - role of maintenance personnel in compressor panel maintenance
   - interface between maintenance and operations personnel

2. **Principles of Configuration**
   - alarm classes (A, B, b, C)
     - purpose and rationale for each class
     - method of configuration/logic loops
   - explanation of compressor startup, operation, and shutdown as a demonstration of how alarm classes function (both manually and due to shutdowns)

3. **Theory of Operation**
   - systems (pneumatic)
     - air supply
     - end devices
     - pneumatic loops
     - panel displays
   - systems (electronic)
     - power supply
     - end devices
     - wiring loops
     - panel displays

4. **Panel Layout and Design**

5. **Maintenance**
   - installation of new/replacement of existing panel devices (pneumatic and electronic)
     - placement
     - interface
     - determination of operating parameters
     - installation considerations
   - calibration
     - frequency
     - decision making for calibration settings
     - calibration procedures (checklist?)
     - safety

6. **Troubleshooting (separate sections for pneumatic and electronic systems)**
   - symptoms
   - probable causes
   - troubleshooting methodology
   - possible solutions
   - safety

7. **Documentation**
   - how to read panel prints
   - process of documenting/updating panel maintenance logs
   - site-specific parameters (Appendix at end of module)

Appendix
   - site-specific settings and parameters for all compressor panels

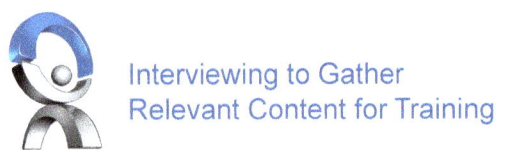
Interviewing to Gather
Relevant Content for Training

ATTACHMENT 5

Shot Sheet

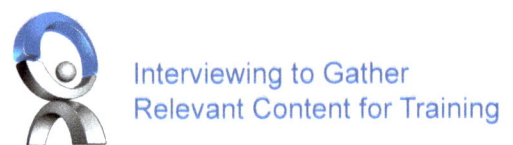

Interviewing to Gather Relevant Content for Training

Attachment 5
Shot Sheet

Company _____ Location _____ Consultant _____

Frame	Description	f/Stop	Shutter Speed
1	Compressor panel C-101	4	125
2	Compressor panel C-101	2.8	125
3	Compressor panel C-102	4	125
4	Compressor panel C-102	2.8	125
5	ESD panel		

SAMPLE

ATTACHMENT 6

Relevant Content Questions

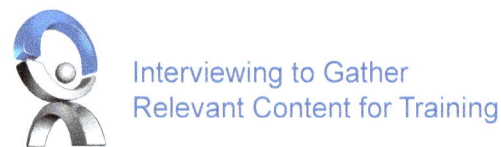

Interviewing to Gather
Relevant Content for Training

Attachment 6
Relevant Content Questions

General Optimization and Loss Control Questions

- Are there any safety issues before, during, or after performing the task?
- What is most important to doing this task effectively?
- How can the worker harm the equipment?
- How can the worker optimize the performance of the equipment?
- How can the worker make the most use of the materials?
- How can the materials be damaged?
- How can the environment be threatened?
- How can the worker best do the task to contribute to the overall job and business success?
- What are the reasons for...?
- What causes...?
- What are the consequences?
- What are the indicators for...?
- What is the worker's response if...?

Prevent Illness and Injury (Safety)

- Does the work involve hazardous materials?
- Does the work involve objects, motion, or force that could cause harm?
- Does the work involve non-ambient conditions that could cause harm?
- Is current or static electricity a factor in doing the work?
- Is radiation present when doing the work?
- Could changes lead to or create a hazardous situation?
- Are there any conditions, actions, or events that can lead to or create a hazardous situation?
- What are the potential consequences of the hazardous situation?
- What controls can be put in place to reduce the probability of an incident occurring and/or the severity of consequences?

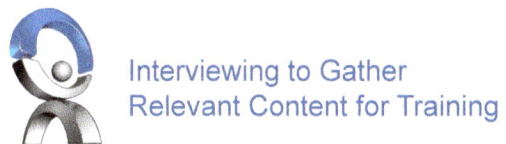

Interviewing to Gather Relevant Content for Training

Attachment 6
Relevant Content Questions

Protect the Environment

- Can this material cause harm to the environment?
- How do I store this material safely?
- How do I dispose of this material safely?
- How much material can be released, disposed of, or harvested without harming the environment?
- How are pollutant releases measured or monitored?
- What technical controls are being used to limit environmental impact?
- How do I know release rates are being exceeded?
- What do I do if release rates are exceeded?
- What do I do if there is a spill of material that has the potential to harm the environment?

Output–Input–Process Variables

Output
- What output variables define the quality of results?
- How are the output variables measured?
- What is the impact of the output materials on PEMEO and vice versa?

Input
- What are the input variables?
- What input variables are changed by the work or technical process?
- What input variables must not change?
- For each variable, is it static or dynamic, controllable or non-controllable?

Process (work or technical)
- What process variables change the materials?
- Are the process variables that change the materials static or dynamic, controllable or non-controllable?
- Which process variables can downgrade the materials?
- How can the materials affect equipment condition and life?
- How can the equipment be operated to perform effectively and efficiently?

Change in variables
- How do I know an output, input, or process variable has changed?
- How does the change affect PEMEO?
- What do I do if a variable changes?

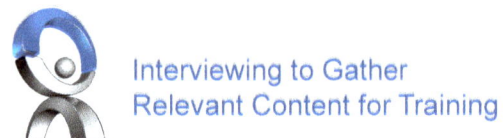

Interviewing to Gather
Relevant Content for Training

Attachment 6
Relevant Content Questions

General Performance Questions
• What job performance issues are critical to the organization? • What is critical to doing the work in a way that contributes to business performance? • Does the worker need to know this to do the work to the established standards? • Are there any business strategies that affect how and how well the work has to be done?

Performance
What has to be done • Who does the work? • What has to be done? • What created the need to do the task? • What conditions affect doing the task? • What materials are required? • What tools and equipment are needed? • Where is the task being done? • When must the task be done? **How it has to be done** • Is there more than one way of performing the task? • Why would one method be better than others? • Why is this step of the procedure done this way? • Is there a risk of people getting ill or injured? • Could the environment be damaged? • Could tools, equipment, and materials get damaged? • How much waste is acceptable? • What can go wrong if: 　− The step was performed poorly? 　− The equipment does not respond as expected? • Is there a need for communication and coordination? **How well it has to be done** • How well am I to do the task? • How do I know that I have done the task satisfactorily? • How do I know that I have done a major step satisfactorily? • How do I know that I have completed this step satisfactorily? • Why must this equipment be operated at this setpoint or within this range?

(continued)

Interviewing to Gather Relevant Content for Training

Attachment 6
Relevant Content Questions

Performance

Reasons, Effects, Consequences
- Why is this task important?
- Why are the steps to a task performed in this order?
- Why must these steps be performed in a specific way?
- Why are these specific safety precautions taken?
- Why did the event occur?
- Why does the internal customer require this work assignment to be completed on schedule?
- Why is this variable important for product quality?

Causes, Effects, Consequences

Ask *What if...?* questions about PEMEO to identify immediate effects and then determine the consequences:
- Could the worker or others become ill and/or injured?
- Could the environment or public be affected?
- Could property, equipment, or materials be damaged?
- What can the worker do to minimize the possibility of an incident occurring and/or the severity of the consequences?
- What should be the worker's first response if an incident occurs?

Work Variables

- Which variables are important to the job?
- Why are the variables important? (reason)
- What are the desirable specifications for the variables?
- Which variables can be controlled?
- Which variables can change?
- Why does a variable change? (reason or cause)
- What if PEMEO does **not** perform as expected—what are the immediate effects?
- What are the indicators that a variable has changed?
- What happens when a variable changes? (consequences for PEMEO)
- What must be done in response to a change in a variable? (reasons, limits of authority)
- How do work processes (operations and maintenance) affect the variables? (consequences for PEMEO)
- What are the worker's roles and responsibilities if the consequences for PEMEO are immediate and severe? (i.e., the desired response to an abnormal or emergency situation)

A6-5

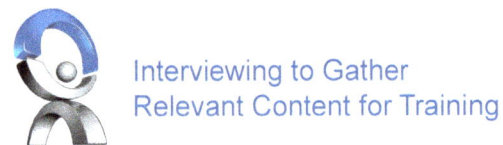

Interviewing to Gather Relevant Content for Training

Attachment 6
Relevant Content Questions

Technical Variables

- What can cause the variable to change?
- What happens when the variable changes?
- What is the acceptable range or set point for the variable?
- What should the worker do if the variable changes?
- Why would the worker want to change the variable?
- Does the worker have control over the variable?
- Does the worker have the authority to change the variable?
- How does the worker change the variable?
- What is the impact on PEMEO if the variable is/is not changed?

Training

- Is this training within the worker's roles and responsibilities?
- Does the worker need to know this to do the work safely, effectively, and efficiently?
- Does the worker already know this because of his or her work experience, education, or prerequisite training?
- Can the worker complete the work satisfactorily by referring to other documents (e.g., equipment specification manual)?
- Does the training record help the supervisor assign work, training, and practice opportunities?
- Should the trainee complete a knowledge test and/or perform tasks on the job as a demonstration of competence?
- What task must the trainee perform?
- How often must the task be performed?
- What are the pre-conditions that require the task to be performed?
- Under what conditions must the task be performed?
- How difficult is it to carry out the task?
- What are the major steps to carrying out the task?
- Are there any critical issues when performing the task that can affect PEMEO?
- How well must the task be performed?
- How do you know the task is performed satisfactorily?
- What are the consequences if the task is not completed, or if the task is not completed satisfactorily?
- What information does the worker need to make decisions in the best interest of the organization?
- Does this information help the worker make decisions?

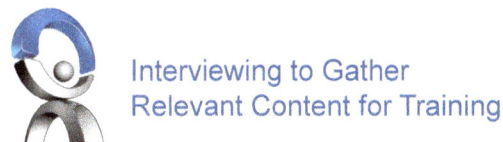

Interviewing to Gather
Relevant Content for Training

Attachment 6
Relevant Content Questions

Developing an Outline for Gathering Content

- What are the main components of the process?
- How does it work?
- What are the major steps for completing the task?
- If we divided the content into these sections, would it work for the trainee?

Other books by Gordon D. Shand:

The Exemplary Worker Book Series

SafeThink™ ...to prevent illness and injury

SafeThink is a structured critical thinking strategy you can use to identify, predict, and control hazardous situations before, during, and after completing work. This cognitive-based safety strategy can be used on the fly, at work, at home, at play, and while driving. *SafeThink* also provides strategies for you to remain focused on your tasks.

WorkThink™ ...to achieve excellent results

WorkThink is a thinking strategy you can use to achieve quality results with the least amount of effort. It usually takes little extra effort to do quality work instead of inferior work. *WorkThink* also emphasizes understanding the expectations of your supervisor, team leader, and customers so that you can achieve the excellent results they expect.

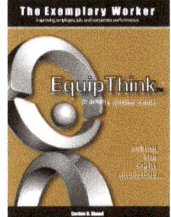

EquipThink™ ...to achieve optimal results

EquipThink is a thinking strategy for you to use tools, mobile equipment, and stationary equipment effectively and efficiently. The goals are for you to achieve the desired results with minimal stress on equipment, to conserve energy, and to extend equipment life. The input–process–output thinking strategy, in conjunction with identifying critical variables, is used to achieve optimal results.

MatThink™ ...to optimize materials

MatThink is a thinking strategy you can use to make the most effective use of materials. The thinking strategy applies to recovering, processing, modifying, applying, transporting, and storing materials. Because equipment and materials are usually closely related, the input–process–output thinking strategy, in conjunction with identifying critical variables, is used to optimize material recovery and use.

EnviroThink™ ...to protect the environment

Both industry and individuals have a responsibility to protect the environment. *EnviroThink* is a critical thinking strategy you can use to identify and respond to environmental issues for any job position that you might hold. *EnviroThink* helps you think through your work by asking yourself specific questions relating to environmental issues important to organizations.

JobThink™ ...to contribute to job and corporate performance

Exemplary workers understand what is important to their organizations. They know the issues critical to business success and where to focus their efforts. *JobThink* addresses the critical thinking strategies you can use to identify what is important for job and corporate performance.

MetaThink™ ...for exemplary performance

MetaThink applies some of the thinking strategies addressed in previous books in different ways and also addresses new thinking strategies useful for the workplace. You can use these thinking strategies, along with the detailed thinking strategies addressed in other books of this series, to achieve exemplary performance.